BIBLE CAVALCADE

BIBLE CAVALCADE

by

H. F. MATHEWS, M.A., B.D.

*(Lecturer in Religious Education, Cheshire County
Training College, Alsager)*

LONDON : EPWORTH PRESS

THE EPWORTH PRESS
(FRANK H. CUMBERS)
25-35 City Road, London, E.C.1

MELBOURNE   CAPE TOWN
NEW YORK   TORONTO

SET IN MONOTYPE BASKERVILLE AND PRINTED IN
GREAT BRITAIN BY THE CAMELOT PRESS LTD
LONDON AND SOUTHAMPTON

PREFACE

No AGE has been richer in books about the Bible than ours, and some excuse must be offered for adding to their number. It is that most of us make the acquaintance of the Bible characters piecemeal, whether at school or in Church worship: but it is through these real people that God has been making Himself known to us for four thousand years. This book does not pretend to go into deep questions of authorship or criticism, but it sets out simply to bring the procession of witnesses in an orderly fashion against the backcloth of their history, so that we may see the ever-growing reality of what God is saying to us.

There is nothing original in these pages. They owe everything to other people—authors and tutors who have made me see something of the rich mine they have explored. My immeasurable debt to them will be partially repaid if any who read these chapters are sent to the big books which contain their treasure.

I am most grateful to my friends, the Revs. John T. Jones, M.A., and William F. Hewitson, B.A., B.D., who read the manuscript and helped me by their comments, and to Mr J. M. Harrison of Alsager Training College who kindly drew the maps which appear at the end.

H. F. M.

June 1953

Contents

Seeing It Whole

MOST of us were introduced to the stories of the Bible almost as soon as we could talk. We heard of the birth of a wonder Child in a manger before we heard about Santa Claus, and we knew something about Noah's Ark before ever we had learned to chatter about Three Blind Mice. Ever since then we have been reading the Bible, or hearing it read. If we have been in the habit of going to church regularly, we have found that Christian worship systematically and consistently relies upon the statements it contains and the narratives with which those statements are closely associated. But if we have never darkened the doors of a church we have still been brought into regular and close contact with the contents of the Bible. Literature is steeped in biblical allusion; music achieves its highest expression when it is linked with words of Scripture. In the morning the BBC usually arranges for us to hear a few verses of the Bible read as an introduction to the day's broadcasting, and frequently programmes end with some form of religious epilogue which normally is based upon something biblical.

In any case we go to school, and the present Education Act lays down that every day shall include a common act of worship, and regular religious instruction shall be given in every county school. Every child receives that instruction unless his parents for conscientious reasons request his withdrawal from such teaching. The result is that, by the time we reach the sixth form, we have come into close contact with the material which makes up the biblical literature for a period of not less than ten years.

During that time, much of the ground will have been covered more than once. Unless the teacher is skilful, as each Scripture period opens we are tempted to shrug our shoulders and mutter: 'Oh, I've heard all this a dozen times before.' This may be quite true of much of what we hear—and it is fully intended that we *should* hear it more than once. We are meant to understand something further of the significance of it on every successive acquaintance with it.

That principle does not exactly apply in other subjects of the school curriculum. When we first learn to multiply, we are dependent upon books of tables and may consult them, or at least run over them silently as we use them. But the time soon comes when we are expected to *know* those tables and to use them almost without thinking about them. A senior boy is rightly insulted if he is asked to go back to look up his tables, or his lists of tense-formations in foreign languages. He should by then have discarded the systematizations of elementary knowledge, because they have become part of his stock-in-trade as a scholar. But we shall be expected to read the story of the Prodigal Son or the Good Shepherd in practically the same form when we are sixteen as we did when we were six.

The fact is, of course, that the arithmetical tables or the conjugations of simple verbs always have the same significance. We may use them in the easiest calculation or the most abstruse mathematical problem, to translate the simplest phrase about 'the teacher has the pen of my aunt', or to render some difficult idiomatic expression in advanced prose. But our Scripture knowledge is being woven into the developing pattern of our moral life. The six-year-old who is first told the story of the Good Samaritan regards it simply as a tale about human kindness, which is a quality he is coming to understand and to appreciate. But when we read the same story in our 'teens', all sorts of problems emerge which mean nothing to the six-year-old. What is my responsibility for other men? How far are race distinctions marring modern life? Is not forgiveness the most difficult virtue to learn, especially when it means forgiving one who is in close relationship with us? At this stage, the Bible is rightly used in schools as a reference book by which we may judge our standards as Christian people.

Again, Scripture-teaching wisely and of set purpose jumps about from Old Testament to New. No teacher starts with the five-year-old at the beginning of Genesis and works steadily through until the adolescent has reached the end of Revelation. Probably during most school years there will be some attempt to study a part of the Old Testament and a part of the New. The year's work may consist of the Age of the Prophets and the Early Growth of the Christian Community, or the Teaching of Jesus and the stories of the Early Kings of Israel. That is all very sound practice, but it means that we have to keep on our toes to realize that there is a tremendous historical gap between these different periods. The gap between early prophets and early Church, for example, is as great as the gap between Chaucer and Chesterton. I always feel that the early stories of Genesis cannot be understood until a boy reaches the fifth form, but no one can prevent him hearing those stories long before he has reached that age. There are stories in the Old Testament which will give him a very unhappy idea of religion unless they are treated carefully and seen in perspective; and until he has reached that age he is likely to be considerably disturbed even by a New Testament story like that of Ananias and Sapphira in Acts 5, no matter how much care successive teachers take to explain it to him.

In any case the division between Old and New Testaments is somewhat artificial. We distinguish between days before Jesus and days after Him, but all is part of the declaration of what God has been saying to men since first they began to apprehend His being and His will. If we are to know anything of the Christian religion, we must recognize that God has been speaking through the whole, and that the whole adds up to the most significant body of religious truth in the world. It is partly true to say that the New Testament 'fulfils' the Old, in the sense that it completes its tendencies and ideas. But it is only partly true. For the revelation in Christ was something complete in itself and startlingly and entirely new: God had never spoken just like this before. 'Unique' is the only word by which it can be described; though even Christ must be seen against the background of the religious development of His people.

Thus it is important that we should piece together the different chunks of biblical knowledge which we have learned and get a complete picture of the whole. This book is an attempt to indicate the general lines upon which such a piecing-together ought to take place. It cannot, of course, deal with all the contents of this majestic library of Christian truth. But it will show how the main parts of the great tradition fit into a whole. The Bible is saying one thing to us. It is not just a record of many events which have happened in the past. It speaks still as the Word of God to us—in what sense we shall presently have to see.

This process of piecing together is not nearly so simple as at first appears. If you have a jig-saw puzzle with a hundred pieces, you can complete the picture by joining contiguous frets which your sense of shape will recognize. You may be helped, too, by the copy of the complete picture which appears on the lid of the box. But the Bible is no jig-saw puzzle. When in the last paragraph I used the metaphor of completing the picture, I did not mean that it was the jig-saw kind of picture. Rather is it an artist's picture. In a great landscape painting there is exquisite beauty in every tree and almost every leaf of every tree. But the artist did not mean us only to admire the craftsmanship of individual parts of his picture. He wanted us to stand back from it and see it whole—and see the truth which he was using his art to portray. Something within us ought to respond to the true beauty of a great painting; and similarly something within us ought to respond to the Bible as a whole.

It follows that the Bible will come to mean more to the man who systematically and conscientiously studies it than to the man who is content to use it as a reference book in a haphazard sort of way. No doubt certain passages stand out more than others, and we find ourselves turning again and again to Isaiah 53, to Paul's hymn about 'love' in 1 Corinthians 13, to some of the perfect parables of Jesus. No doubt we may find help in our devotional life by 'dipping' into the Bible almost at random or by following a course of passages prepared because they all bear on a particular topic. There are similar highlights in the landscape we were just considering. But the man who gets most out of the Bible is he who is prepared to give it hard and disciplined study. He will find that God is saying something through the Bible as a whole which makes it the unique volume of religion which it is. There is, indeed, a unity in the Bible which forces itself upon us as we consider it whole. Even though it covers the most diverse phases of history, that unity persists. We start with the record of a few Semitic tribesmen wandering between the two great civilizations of the Euphrates and the Nile, and we end with the emergence of a small but astonishingly virile new society of those who believed in the Resurrection, comprising men of all races and colours, slaves and freemen, rich and poor, grown into a force which was destined to undermine the paganism of the mighty Roman Empire. But in it all God is saying some one thing to us. We realize what Coleridge meant when he said that there was something in the Bible which 'found' him. It is for us to seek in that all-pervading unity what is God's message for *us*. We, like the Israelites, set out in life looking for a promised land; and, like the Israelites, we often find that our ambition has carried us toward a disturbing warfare rather than to a sequestered peace. We, as well as the Israelites, are tempted to go after false gods (though ours may not be represented by wood or stone as theirs were), and find—like them—that only the providence of God saves us from disaster. Our own consciences confirm the truth of the biblical story of Adam and Eve that man mars the image of God within himself by his own pride and self-sufficiency. We—and not only the first disciples—find that Jesus has always some challenge which is beyond our standards. Therefore the whole Bible has a *meaning* for us which we can only discover gradually as we live into the whole history of God's dealings with men which it outlines.

It is not easy for us to realize that the Bible grew gradually out of the Church. There was no 'blue-print'. No one planned a collection of diverse literary essays which might be put together to help people to live properly. As Hebrew—and later, Christian—people marvelled at what God had done for them and in them, they felt impelled to record in different ways their impressions of the meaning of this divine impact upon history. Gradually one after another of these writings was used in the community, and so achieved a sort of authority because it helped other people in their problems. In course of time a norm or 'canon' of writings which could be regarded as scriptural came to be commonly accepted (though we cannot be sure when this happened either for Old Testament or New. We only know that the books we recognize as belonging to the Old Testament were recognized by the time of the Council of Jamnia, at the end of the first century A.D., and the exact collection which we accept as the New Testament was first definitely recorded in the Paschal Letter of Athanasius as late as A.D. 367). It is clear, then, that the underlying unity we have been speaking about is no man-made arrangement. The Bible is a unity because it is the record of God's action.

The clue to the understanding of what the Bible really is will be found in the meaning of the word we have already used several times to describe the two parts—Jewish and Christian—into which the Bible is naturally divided. I mean the word 'testament'. In the Old Testament we frequently meet the idea of 'covenant'. God made His covenant with Israel. One king made a covenant with another. 'Covenant' and 'testament' represent the same word. Jesus spoke of the wine at the Last Supper as His 'blood of the covenant' which was shed for His friends. A covenant was an agreement or contract between two parties. In its primitive form, it was simply a bargain between two men; and often they would seal the bargain by dabbing each other with a drop of blood from a nicked vein: that was the earliest form of receipt. Later it came to mean a treaty between States. When we speak of a covenant between man and God we mean that there is set up a relationship between them on the basis of man's obedience. The Almighty God announces His terms—moral loyalty to His revealed will. Those who accept His terms find that God stands in a unique relationship with them which makes life entirely different.

So the Scriptures of the Old and New Testaments are the records of that agreement. On the one side, they are the authoritative statement of the demands of God to those who wish to be His men; and on the other side they are the record of the way in which God established relations between men and Himself. Dr Dodd says that the Scriptures 'are the charter defining the status of the Church as the people of God, the terms upon which that status is granted, and the obligations it entails'.[1]

That is what we are trying to trace in this book. In one sense, the study of Scripture helps us to have a standard by which we measure our moral actions and thoughts. Our code of conduct is indeed based upon the Bible—not only upon the Ten Commandments, but upon the Bible as a whole, so that we should ask ourselves how everything we do or think appears in relationship to the will of God. But in another sense the Bible is a much bigger book than that. It is the title-deed to the Kingdom of God. To possess it, and to understand its true significance, is to enter on a unique heritage. It is to be an heir. There is a fortune for the claiming.

[1] *The Bible Today,* p. 8.

CHAPTER ONE

The People and the Book

CHRISTIANS, then, are people of a Book. Their religion is bound up with the Bible—a collection of religious documents written between 1800 and 2800 years ago. Other religions have had their sacred books—the Mohammedan Koran, the Hindu Vedas, the five King Books of Confucianism. But the Christian Bible is quite different from any one of them and serves a different purpose. By contrast, the Koran is a book rather shorter than our New Testament, consisting of 114 discourses of Mohammed, which were collected after his death by the prophet's secretary (for Mohammed himself could neither read nor write). To the Moslem it represents the very words of God spoken to His people through His prophet; but if we take an English translation we shall find it wearisome reading.

That could never be said about the Bible. It has often been pointed out that the Bible contains some of the world's finest poetry, noblest law, highest culture, deepest thought, and sublimest drama. In literary value alone it has achieved a place supreme among all the classics of the English tongue. It enshrines the highest religious aspirations and achievements of the human race. It speaks with a voice more authoritative than that of any other volume in the world. But when all that has been said, we have not yet hit upon the reason why it is unique in the world's religious literature.

In the Bible 'God has given us a book full of stories'. It is packed from cover to cover with real people, characters who stand out vividly as the real individuals they

B

were. Our religion is taught to us in the experience of
men and women who lived at various times during a
period of close on two thousand years. When the ancient
Greeks wanted to teach their children about religion,
they recited the ancient myths about the gods who dwelt
on Mount Olympus; but we learned our religion from
stories about real human people and how they came to
believe in God.

The pictures the Bible paints are pictures of folk we can
identify and understand. Read through that story again
in Acts 9 of Saul of Tarsus, the rabidly enthusiastic
persecutor who went with official commission to Damascus. He was in an emotional state of mind, caused by his
uncertainty whether Jesus was not after all the promised
Messiah who had been crucified by some tragic misunderstanding. But let your eyes wander on farther in
the story. Go through the city gate at Damascus and
down the evil-smelling streets until you find the house of
Ananias. Poor wretch! You hardly expect to find him
asleep, for the news has come on in advance that to-
morrow Saul will be there, and the life of a professing
follower of this Jesus will not then be worth much. But
Ananias has a vision, in which he is told to go direct to
Saul's lodging. It does not take much to understand his
protestations. He has heard from many the kind of thing
Saul does when he gets to work. Go to him? Would that
not be to court disaster? Let your imagination track him
as he makes his way reluctantly to Straight Street (there
is a narrow street in the modern town of Damascus still
called by its ancient name), and passes and re-passes the
house of Judas before he finally plucks up courage to
knock. We learn more from such stories about what their
religion meant to men like Ananias than from pages of
dissertation about its theology.

Of quite another sort is the matchless story in 2 Samuel

23$^{13-17}$. David, outlaw chief but popular hero, is encamped in his cave at Adullam. The Philistine tribesmen are his people's natural foes and the skirmishes have been going on for days in the hot season. They are almost worn out with fatigue of battle, but each of David's men would give his life if his leader demanded it. What would David not give to be back in the good old peaceful days of his shepherd life at Bethlehem? As he sinks down in the cave at night, he gives vent to his longing for the Philistines to be ousted from his native town so that he can once again taste the water from the well in his home town. So three of his merry men, taking their leader at his word, slip away secretly by night and return bearing a cup of precious water from Bethlehem, stolen from the enemy stronghold. Other men of ancient and more recent times have shown loyalty as great as that; but the end of the story is that David declares this water to be sacred. It rightly belongs to God, for it has been brought at the risk of men's lives; and there is for us high religious value in the story when we see in David's sacrificial action the expression of his faith in the unseen Leader of all Israel's enterprises.

They are real stories—stories about real people and their successes and failures, their hopes and aspirations. They are men like ourselves, and through them God speaks to us. God is active in history, and in the particular history covered by the Bible God reveals Himself. Twenty-six times in the Bible He is called 'the living God', by which phrase the writers imply that God is taking the initiative all through. When we use the word 'history' we do not mean merely a succession of events. We imply that those events are in some way related. There is a meaning in the events for someone. If there had been no meaning, the events would never have been recorded or remembered. So far as biblical history is concerned, its meaning all the way through is that God and man meet. Not only is God revealed in nature—in the beauty of the world which He made. As a matter of fact, the Bible contains less than we should expect about nature as an evidence for the existence of God. God transcends nature. Continually in the pages of the Bible we are made aware of a supernatural power revealed through the happenings it records. Partly, it is true, the Bible is the record of man's search for God. But, just as Adam and Eve hid from God when (as the exquisite picture-story naïvely puts it) God walked in the garden in the cool of the evening, so do many of us avoid the divine encounter. The Bible is first and foremost the account of His search for man. It is the record of the Eternal breaking into human life at a thousand points.

The biblical writers often use the metaphor 'the Word of God' to express the reality of this encounter. We are not meant only to think of God speaking in a physical form, of course. But when one man speaks to another, he invites a response. The other is perfectly free to reject his approach, or even to ignore him altogether. But he may be affected fundamentally by what is said to him. Something of that kind is implied by the phrase 'the Word of God'. God leaves us free to respond as we will, but He has taken the initiative. As we see the meaning of the Bible story, an obligation is laid upon us to act. The parable of the Good Samaritan has meaning for *us*, as well as for the scribe to whom Jesus said: 'Go thou and do likewise.'

All the way through the Bible God chooses to speak to us through men. We recognize that fact when we think of the prophets, for they were announcing things in the name of Jehovah. But the Hebrew also looked upon the laws, enunciated by men like Moses, as the Word of God. To put it another way, law and history are equally means of God's unveiling of Himself to His people. (In the Jewish Bible books like Genesis and Exodus, which are partly historical, are actually included in the main section entitled 'Law', because all history was regarded as the working out of God's law for men.) In the New Testament, we expect to find much of importance for our faith in the letters of Paul, for there he works out in words what the Christian religion really means. But most of us find even more of the meaning of Christianity in the account in the Acts of the Apostles of the actual adventures of the first men who named Jesus as Lord. That is of intense religious value to us simply because it is the record of God's dealings with ordinary, fallible men.

This is why Jesus spoke in parables. He might have worked out for us a complete statement of who God is and laid down for all time exactly what men should believe about Him. He might have drawn up a completely new code of laws, so that we could go to them today and find precisely what constitutes right or wrong behaviour. But that was not His way. Instead He told stories; for He knew that people remember stories when instructions have been long forgotten. Of course, other teachers had used parables. There are many of them still extant which the rabbis used in their preaching, but the parables of Jesus stand on an altogether different plane from those of the rabbis. They strike us immediately as more real, and, if we examine them in any detail, we shall soon see what that difference is. It is that the parables which Jesus told are about people—real people. All the pictures are so true to life that we can recognize in them the laws which Jesus intended men to obey far more adequately than if He had laid them down with literal exactitude; and the nature of God is far clearer to us than it would have been if He had proclaimed with the most powerful oratory that God was omnipotent, eternal, 'slow to anger and plenteous in mercy'.

Put in another way, this is to say that the Bible revelation is given through personality. That is true of the Old Testament as well as the New. Take away the great figures of the Israelite race—Abraham, Moses, Elijah, Amos, Jeremiah, Josiah, Judas the Maccabee—and the Old Testament loses most of its meaning. We see God through their adventure of living; and God speaks to us through the story of their lives. But there is an important corollary to that. Unless we understand something of the relationship between the different people in the Bible, we cannot rightly estimate the value we should put on any particular incident or character. We obviously do not expect to find the same help and guidance from the life of Elijah, who lived in the ninth century B.C., as from the life of the apostle Paul. Nor do we think the lists of names of the tribesmen which appear in Numbers are worthy to be placed in the same category as the teaching of Jesus in John's Gospel. In other words, before we can rightly appreciate the Bible, we must know something of the history of the people who appear in it and of the processes by which that story came to be recorded for us to read.

We have grown up to honour and respect this Book. We have read it and listened to it being read in school, in church, and in our own homes. We can say that we have some acquaintance with the stories it relates and a general knowledge of the main events in the lives of the greatest characters it portrays. Moreover, many of us have found that it has a value in public worship and in private devotion that we cannot easily express in words, but which we should be loth to surrender. Its matchless prose has become the standard by which good English may be judged, and many of its phrases have entered into our common language; but that is by no means all.

There were days when the Bible was valued chiefly as giving authoritative replies to all the possible questions about life which men could ask. I remember a woman who had what she called a 'promise box'. It consisted of two or three hundred little pieces of paper each rolled up and stood on end in a little cardboard box; and on each piece of paper there was a text from some part or other of the Bible. When she was in doubt or trouble, she could take out any piece of paper at random and often find help and comfort in the words it contained. Not for all the world would I decry that woman's faith, for she lived very near to God; but I suggest there is another, and I believe a better, way of realizing the meaning of the Bible for men of this and every age.

Within these covers are masterpieces of poetry, tragedy, history, and philosophy. But if I am studying any literature—a play of Shakespeare, a novel of Thomas Hardy, a poem of William Blake, or a philosophical treatise of Aristotle—I shall obviously get far more out of it if I can read it against the background of its author's age and the times about which and for which he was writing. It seems logical to suppose therefore that the Bible will be considerably enhanced in value for us if we can get a general picture of the background against which it was written. Most of us have gained through the years a knowledge of much of that which goes to make up this Bible. We have browsed among its stories: its heroes and seers have made their own impressions upon us. But we need to see the Bible as a whole, and its people as actors in one great drama, which extends through the centuries. The fact is that God has been making Himself known to men all through history, and so, in order to discover for ourselves what He has been saying, we must see the literature of His people as the mirror which reflects His ways with them.

Like every other science, that of literary criticism has in the last century progressed by leaps and bounds. At first this science, again like all other sciences, disturbed people rather than helped them. But that phase has passed. We have grown up to use physics and chemistry to serve our countless needs, and we may do the same with the science of biblical criticism. We cannot all be experts in subjects which have occupied the entire lives of some of the world's finest intellects, but we can at least enter into the heritage which they have passed on to us, and benefit from their researches in the same way as we benefit from the discovery of electricity, wireless, or radium. By assimilating some of the findings which great scholars have generously made common property, the Bible can become immeasurably more real and of infinitely greater value to us. It is needless to say that in these pages only hints can be given of the main lines of the growth of literature and the moral and spiritual growth of God's people, but there are many good books which deal more adequately with each section of the subject.

The history of the period which is covered by the Bible shows two main processes at work—the gradual unveiling of the nature and purpose of God until we see Him 'face to face' in Jesus Christ, and the long, slow process by which men came to discover Him in all His fullness and His meaning for their lives.

It is often said that the Bible is 'inspired'. It would be more accurate to say that the authors received inspiration for their work. That is to say, they felt an inward urge to declare what they had felt and seen in the realm of religion. To some of them, that urge came in a prophetic vision and with ecstatic experience which is quite foreign to our understanding today; whilst to others it came as a result of a straightforward reasoning process.

For instance, the prophet Isaiah in a moment of high vision 'saw the Lord high and lifted up and his train filled the Temple', and he felt compelled to declare what he had experienced. Mark, on the other hand, having followed Peter in his missionary tours, came to see that when Peter was dead people would need to have some authentic account of what Jesus did on earth. But we cannot say that he was not inspired to write his gospel because it was the result of his reasoning. Bernard Shaw makes Joan reply to her inquisitor who sneers at her visions and says that they are merely her imagination: 'Of course. That is how the messages of God come to us.'

Naturally some of the writers were more conscious of a sense of inspiration than others, and hence their writings differ considerably in religious value for us. It so happens that the Book of Esther does not mention the name of God, and we seldom read it either in public or in private. But that does not make it completely worthless. It may be true that its writer was not very much 'inspired', but it is of relative value to us in trying to assess the religious ideas of the people of the time, and in seeing how much the people had learned of the nature of God.

The order of the books of our English Bibles is rather confusing. The Old Testament is arranged in four successive sections—Law, History, Poetry, and Prophets. The Prophets include the three great rolls of prophetic oracles —Isaiah, Jeremiah, and Ezekiel—and the Book of the Twelve Minor Prophets; and in the Hebrew Scriptures the historical books (Joshua—Kings) were included in this section as the 'Former Prophets', because they cover the period during which the earlier prophets were active. In the New Testament the four gospels are placed in an order which gives quite a false impression of the order in which they were written; and they are followed by the Acts and then the Epistles in an arbitrary order, and the Revelation. As we work through the history we shall try to set the books of the Bible in their historical perspective so that they can declare their full meaning to us. At the end we may come to find that the Bible has achieved a new authority for us by inducing in us a sense of the unity of God's revelation of Himself. We shall be able to feel our part in the army of men and women of all the ages to whom God has revealed something of the truth about Himself, and that realization may bring us very near to Him.

Questions for Discussion

1. What is the difference between the inspiration of a book and the inspiration of a man?
2. Consider what use the Old Testament is to people who are followers of Jesus.
3. Which do you think is the most dramatic story in the Bible? Discuss its value as a means of teaching religion.
4. Why do preachers usually commence their sermons with a 'text'?
5. What do you mean by 'the literary value of the Bible'?

CHAPTER TWO

Camp-Fire Wisdom

ONE OF the things which make life so much worth living is the fact that we know so little. The mind of man was made to explore the universe in which he came to live, and the mine of knowledge is so deep and its store so vast that we are never likely to exhaust its possibilities. We were born to ask questions, more particularly questions about ourselves and our place in the gigantic scheme of things. In that sense we are all scientists—for science seeks to explore and to formulate the knowledge man gains about himself and his world. Just as we learned far more in childhood by asking questions than by listening to people telling us what *they* thought we ought to know, so in the childhood of the race—'when the world was very young'—our ancestors sought the answers to their questions from the wise men of the tribe. Thus the first 'knowledge' came to be—the sum of the wisdom of those to whom men looked for guidance, the tribal leaders or sheiks.

How did the world start? Where did we come from? How came there to be human life and animal life and plant life on this planet? These are the questions we started to ask when we were four and five; and these are the questions early men asked. They asked them first as they sat at night round the camp fire which both gave them warmth in the cold eastern night and also kept at bay the wild beasts which would have scattered their flocks and herds if they had not been frightened away by the glow and crackle of burning wood. In the long evenings they found their answers, and these were passed on from generation to generation, father telling son round his camp fire what he had heard from his elders in his youth. We are concerned with the answers given by a specific collection of these tribesmen, the Hebrews. We must remember that they are the answers of people who were very 'young', in the sense that their knowledge was that of a very undeveloped civilization. It was hundreds of years before other men came and collected, edited, and wrote down these answers, for the spoken word was the only means of communication between man and man for many generations. It is because of their work that we are able today to read what early men thought.

Generally speaking, this work of final compilation was not done until after the Babylonian exile. But before that time there had been many attempts at different times to gather together the picture-tales of ancient Israel, and it was from these various collections that the final editors produced the books of the Old Testament as we have them. We may conveniently start with the traditions about the Creation of the world (though we ought to remember that these were not necessarily the earliest of our constituent records). They may not be scientific accounts, but they are not untrue for all that.

The other day I saw a drawing done by a boy in his first term at school. It was meant to represent a man. It was not by any means an accurate drawing. In fact, it consisted mainly of a roundish head, attached by a neck which was not very symmetrical to a body which had a certain amount of connexion with two legs. But it was quite difficult to see how those legs could support the body, or how the arms, which stuck out from the body rather like the limbs of a scarecrow, would have been very much use for anything which required manual skill. But, when one considered how young was the boy who had drawn the figure, there was cause for much commendation. It was not art, but it had the marks of incipient ability, and I shall be surprised if that boy does not produce some really good drawings when he is older. As a portrait of a man, it left much to be desired, but it did convey a number of truths, even though it did not convey the whole truth. I should be able to learn from it that his body was roughly a certain shape, that he possessed hands and feet and wore clothes of a certain kind. But I should not be able to learn from it anything about the character of the man. I cannot find the deep, meaningful portrayal which a famous artist would convey if he were to draw the same figure. In his work I should learn a thousand times as much as from the boy's; but that does not mean that the boy's picture must be dismissed as of no value.

All that is true of the picture of the Creation which Genesis provides. It is not concerned to answer the questions which are asked rightly by geologists and biologists, and will give us no help in solving those problems. It *is* concerned with the more fundamental questions about the reality of God and His dealings with men. In that realm it has something to say which is permanently valid and eternally true. It is a primitive account of things as man first apprehended them in the infancy of human understanding. We learn from it that there are distinct stages in the work of inhabiting the universe with bird and beast, fish and flower, and with man himself. We learn from it the basic truth that all life goes back to God; and even if round the camp fire men in their simplicity explained life by saying that God 'breathed into his nostrils the breath of life; and man became a living soul', this does not deny the truth of the knowledge which has come to us by other means since that early day. Genesis tells us the simple fact that in the background of all life there was God. It does not tell us a great deal about the character of God. That is the discovery and expression of a later stage of human development. So, if we expect from Genesis a learned disquisition on the protoplasmic basis of organic life, we shall be making as absurd a demand as if we expected the exquisite work of Van Gogh from a six-year-old.

There are two accounts of the Creation in the early chapters of Genesis (1^1–2^3, 2^4–3^{24}). They are very different, as you will see. Chapter 1 has for its theme the dependence of man upon God. The wonder and majesty of Nature and the infinitely greater wonder of Man have no meaning at all apart from the God who created and sustains both. Of that Creation, man has the place of honour as the culmination of the purpose of God for His world. The other account (which scholars think is the earlier) is concerned more with the responsibility which comes to man because he is made 'in the image of God'.

Some things are right, others are wrong, and we are so made that we can make our choice between them. Why? Who said what was right and what was wrong? The sage at the camp fire answered that the Lord God (he gave Him a more specific name—the Hebrew title Jehovah—than the general title of the later account—God) who created man demands obedience; for He is supreme arbiter of the moral order as well as of Nature. The story of the Garden of Eden is a word-picture drawn to show how God revealed to men the distinctions of ethics. Behind everything is God. Man was created by Him, and to Him he is responsible for the life he leads. We shall not suppose in our more highly developed state of mind and religion that God literally 'spoke' to a man called Adam in the Garden, or chased him round the trees, calling: 'Where art thou?' That is a pictorial explanation of a real fact—that disobedience to the moral law of the universe produces effects in the divine realm as well as in the human; in other words, that sin concerns God as well as man. It is an incomplete explanation, of course, just as the myth that we believed as children that Father Christmas brought the presents we found in the pillow-case at the end of the bed is an incomplete—and in many ways an unworthy—explanation of the fact that we are dependent upon others for many of life's best gifts.

The problem of man's failure to observe the moral law led to the inclusion of another story in this early collection—the story of the Flood, which is found in most of the literatures of the East and confirms the assertion of the geologists that there was a great deluge which overwhelmed the lands of the Middle East in prehistoric times. Sir Leonard Woolley in 1929 discovered near the site of Ur (Abraham's ancient home) a stratum of perfectly clean clay, eight feet thick, covering remnants of pottery, brick, and implements of pre-Sumerian civilization which he dated as about 3200 B.C. He believes that such a great thickness of clay could only have been deposited by a great flood such as the Bible and Sumerian legends describe.[1] The story of Noah's Ark is early man's attempt to explain how men and animals were left afterwards to people the earth again. The ancient myth-story has very little importance as a geological record, but it cannot be surpassed as a symbolic explanation of the undoubted fact that God's judgement comes upon man's folly, and yet God can overwhelm disaster.

So far we have learned very little about the nature of God other than that He is a powerful creative Spirit who demands obedience. But when we come to the stories of Abraham we come to the beginnings of the history of the people of Israel. The Norse word 'saga' is often used to

[1] *Ur of the Chaldees*, pp. 18-25.

describe the hero-tales associated with Abraham, Isaac, Jacob, and Joseph. These sagas are probably a mixture of history and legend: they record some facts but they are also a medium for conveying primitive ideas to us.

There is no doubt that the Hebrews did come at some time from Babylonia to settle in Palestine. The biblical story explains that Abraham set out from Ur at the command of his God. We are tantalizingly left in ignorance of the political causes or the economic needs which led immediately to such an adventure. Paul suggests in Romans 4[1-3] that Abraham learned something of the nature of God by faithfully obeying Him in every respect. He may not have possessed a complete knowledge of God: who does? but his faith 'was reckoned unto him for righteousness'. That is what all the stories teach which are recorded of him. If Lot, his nephew, had a wife who was caught in the lava from a volcanic eruption, it was because she failed to obey God's command to leave the fated city. On the other hand, because Abraham was even prepared to sacrifice his son Isaac, he became the first man to learn that the commonly accepted practice of child-sacrifice was not consistent with belief in the God he professed to serve. This was one of the greatest civilizing discoveries of all time, and there are occasions later in the Old Testament (for instance in the story of Jephthah in Judges 11[29-40]) when human sacrifice was still practised. In other respects, Abraham still maintained the undeveloped customs of his age. (We should not necessarily think very highly of a father who sent a slave to find a wife for his son, as Abraham sent for Rebekah; but in his day it was the father's right and duty to purchase a wife for his son with presents—'jewels of silver, and jewels of gold, and raiment'—and certainly Isaac was quite satisfied with the deal.) But we feel that Abraham fully deserves the title of Father of the Jewish race which later history gave him, for he marks the first stage in the long process by which God made known to men what was His nature.

By the time Isaac had reached old age the race was ready for its next lesson in constructive morality. His sons Esau and Jacob were a strangely assorted pair, the one a sportsman-adventurer who came to a bad end, the other a scheming scoundrel who yet became so worthy a man that his descendants were reckoned as the Chosen Race. By no possible code of ethics can Jacob's action in depriving his brother of his legitimate birthright be defended, but we know more of him than of Esau because of what he learned when God appeared to him in a dream during his flight. There at the foot of his dream ladder he recognized the fact that man cannot plan his life without taking account of God. Esau never learned that lesson. His life of vengeance was self-inspired. When Jacob cried out, 'Surely the Lord is in this place; and I knew it not . . . this is none other but the house of God, and this is the gate of heaven', he made the first step toward his later declaration, which he ratified by setting up the stone he had used for a pillow as the altar of the first Hebrew shrine at Beth-el: 'If God will be with me . . . then shall the Lord be my God.' It was this fact of realizing his dependence upon God which made him worthy to be the founder of a race whose history should influence the world more than any other. So his name Jacob, which meant 'deceiver', was exchanged for Israel, and his twelve sons gave their names to the twelve tribes which eventually united to form the nation of Israel.

Like most brothers, these sons quarrelled. The general cause of the trouble was Joseph, who, having been spoiled by an indulgent father, fancied that he was a cut above all of them. No one is likely to take kindly to a junior

who boasts that in his dream his brothers' sheaves bow
down to his sheaf. The temptation of getting rid of 'the
Dreamer' by selling him to passing Ishmaelite caravanners
was too much for ordinary men at their stage of development, and it was the matter of a moment to take his coat
of many colours (really a long-sleeved cloak, intended for
a man who had no need to work) and invent a yarn
about a wild beast. But from that point the story ceases
to be the record of men's dealings with each other.
Potiphar, the baker and the butler, the Pharaoh, the
widespread famine which brought the brothers to the
well-stocked granaries where wisdom had made the Egyptians store their surplus, are all portrayed as mere instru-
ments in the hand of God. Joseph's phenomenal rise to
power in Egypt is all God's doing for the benefit of Israel.
There is purpose behind this true story; and the author
is not merely recording what happened to people of a
distant past, but he is recording for all time how God
works within the affairs of men and sometimes overrules
their plans for His own design. In the words which the
early narrative puts into the mouth of Joseph: 'Be not
grieved, nor angry with yourselves, that ye sold me hither:
for God did send me before you to preserve life' (Genesis
45⁵). 'It was not you that sent me hither, but God'
(Genesis 45⁸). Men were beginning to learn His nature
as they told their stories. Is there even a suggestion that
Joseph, having learned to his sorrow how a favourite can
grow up with a distorted view of life, goes out of his way
to teach the new favourite, Benjamin, by the simple expedient of secreting his goblet in his sack, the danger of
his exalted position?

There is no reason why this story of Joseph should not
be the true explanation of the fact that a tribe of Semites
did come to settle in Egypt. Tutmose III refers in an
inscription to places named after Jacob and Joseph; and

archæological evidence suggests that Ramses II employed Semites in the building of Pithom and Ramses, the store-cities, just as the biblical account infers. The position of Jacob and Joseph and their tribes was bound to change in those days of closely guarded racialism, and slavery was the legitimate expectation of nomad tribes within the area of domination of a strong power like Egypt when, as the Bible puts it, 'there arose a new king over Egypt who knew not Joseph'—or, as the Egyptian historical records state, there was a change of politics following the expulsion of the Hyksos (the shepherd-kings of Egypt who were themselves Semites) and the establishment of the eighteenth dynasty.

But, by the time that such a slave-relationship was created, these Hebrew tribesmen had made their first adventures in discovering what God was like. Already religion had become the foundation of their tribal life, and, even if we are inclined to think that religion primitive and unworthy, it is from these early beginnings that our faith in God develops. That is just one of the reasons why we still tell these camp-fire stories.

References

The Creation—Genesis 2^4–3^{24}, 1^1–2^3.

The Flood Story—Genesis 6^5–9^{17}.

Abraham—Genesis 12^{1-9}, 13^{1-18}, 19^{24-8}, 22^{1-19}, 24^{1-67}.

Isaac, Esau, and Jacob—Genesis 27^{1-45}, 28^{10-22}, 32^{3-32}.

Joseph—Genesis 37^{1-36}, $39^{1-6,\ 19-23}$, 40^1–41^{49}, 42^1–46^7, 47^{1-12}.

Questions for Discussion

1. The legend that there was a great flood in the eastern Mediterranean region appears in many ancient mythologies and is confirmed by the researches of

the geologists. In that case, what is the purpose of its inclusion in the Old Testament? Does it add in any way to our knowledge of God?

2. What is there in the stories of Abraham to justify his being called 'the father of the Israelite race'? Do we owe anything to him?

3. What is the importance to the history of religion of the story of God's appearance to Jacob at Beth-el?

4. Suggest two or three reasons why the story of Joseph should find a place in the record of the development of Hebrew religion.

5. Do you think it is right to teach these early stories to young children in school? If so, are there any features which teachers should avoid mentioning in case they give youngsters wrong ideas of religion which they will later have to unlearn?

CHAPTER THREE

The Tribes on Trek

IT WAS from one of the families of these persecuted builder slaves that the deliverer of the people was to come. By a most romantic chance he was saved from death by a combination of astuteness on the part of his mother and a whim of fancy on the part of the princess of the Egyptian court, and so given an Egyptian up-bringing and such education as Egypt provided for her most fortunate sons. Even the name of Moses is Egyptian. It meant 'son'. The Hebrew writer in Exodus 2¹⁰ tried later on to explain it by straining the sound of the Hebrew word which meant 'drawn out', but the presence of Ahmose, Tutmose, and so on, as common Egyptian names in this period, shows that Moses received full adoption as an Egyptian. The well-intentioned accident in which his strength proved greater than he thought is just the kind of thing which would make any man flee the country; and, as was to be expected, Moses reverted to the job his ancestors did—tending sheep for the priest of Midian. But, though Moses could flee from justice, the God who overruled the cruelty of Joseph's brothers was still at hand to take an active interest in the affairs of the race. Some unusual physical phenomenon on one of the rare bushes first attracted the attention of Moses. The splendour of that sight made him worship as many a man has found cause to worship in the sunset. It seemed to him as though the bush was on fire and he was in the very presence of God, and it was the most natural thing in the world to take off his sandals as a token of respect for the holy implications of scene and place. The exile from his people, who had long pondered the wrongs of the race to which he rightly belonged, could hear the very voice of God, as he afterwards explained to the simple people of his time. God called him to a mission—daring, exacting, dangerous. He might argue his unworthiness and inability, but here was a new feature in the relationship between man and God. God would make his tongue-tied speech of use in approaching Pharaoh. Who better than he would know the court and its ways? God would work with him, but he was to be the first of a long line of divine messengers to men.

The plagues which accompanied his demands of Pharaoh were natural happenings, as we should expect; for God, whose hand we are meant to see in them, cannot be false to His own laws. Frogs and lice, flies and locusts are common enough in that land, and the turning of the River Nile into 'blood' presumably represents what has often happened since—the red sandy silt from the source of the river made it undrinkable as the flow of the river became slower. In the pools bred mosquitoes, the cause of much disease. The final catastrophe was the great death which swept through the Egyptian nation. This has all the peculiarities of the bubonic plague which later ravaged Sennacherib's army (see 2 Kings 19[35]), and which is generally admitted to be caused by a germ carried by rats and mice. Perhaps we must assume that there has been some misunderstanding on the part of the editors of our story, who have recorded that it was the firstborn of every Egyptian family (both human and animal) who suffered. That is the natural kind of exaggerative statement which would be made as the story was retailed from father to son.

So the slave tribes escaped from the hand of the oppressor king. In the desert their new-found leader reminded them immediately that their escape was due, not to his genius as leader, but to the hand of the God they must never forget to honour. In token of that fact they ate their first meal together—lamb and unleavened bread, for there had been no time in their hurried collection of belongings to bring the piece of fermented dough which each family used instead of yeast. Every year since, the race has celebrated that Passover feast—named after their simple explanation that the angel of death 'passed over' the Israelite tents—and every year the tradition of the significance of the festival has been preserved; for in each Jewish family the eldest son asks the senior member of the family to explain to them the meaning of the Passover. (see Exodus 12 $^{26-7}$).

The tribesmen completed their escape by crossing the Red Sea. Probably they used the sandy stretch between Suez and the Bitter Lakes where land is only a few feet above sea-level and may have been covered with water in those days which would be readily driven back by the 'strong east wind' which Exodus describes. We can imagine how, when the wind dropped, the Egyptian chariots would be caught in the quicksands. We may be able to find more ordinary explanations of the events which seemed so miraculous to the Israelite editors. Travellers have occasionally observed things which could naturally be described as pillars of cloud and fire. But that does not affect the one great thing which the early stories say —God acted to deliver His people. Later, when food was short, they came across the glucose deposit produced by tamarisk trees at the end of May and beginning of June, which melts in the sun. They called it 'manna'—which in Hebrew meant 'What is it?' God was providing for them in His own way.

So far the tribes seem to have been but loosely united. Moses, with noble insight, made their religion the bond of unity. At one of their frequent halts he left them in order to spend some time on Sinai in meditation with God.

The result was that he presented them with an ultimatum. This was most probably the direct result of the pagan sight he witnessed immediately on his return, for the people had forsaken God for idol-worship. He proposed that they should enter into a bargain-agreement which a simple people, as they were, could understand. The terms were to be that they should distinguish the God they worshipped by a proper name, Jehovah, which may perhaps best be represented in English by Dr Moffatt's phrase, 'The Eternal'; that they should adopt a primitive code of tribal morality (part of this is what we familiarly call the Ten Commandments) similar to that announced by Hammurabi the Babylonian; that they should construct an Ark, or box, to contain the stone tablets on which these laws were inscribed, together with other things to remind them of their relationship with Jehovah; that they should worship Jehovah alone in a tent of meeting, and that He should not be represented by any of the creature shapes which stood for the gods of the other nomad tribes. On His part, Moses declared, God undertook to guide their trek to a successful issue in a 'land of promise'.

To us this does not represent a very high and noble form of religion, but savours of the crudely commercial business-deal—God will look after you if you will worship Him. But in fact it was an infinite advance on the religion of any of the tribesmen who lived in the world of the fifteenth century B.C., and was much more sane and rational than the uncertain hopes and fears of the patriarchs of the earliest days. Moses gave to this agreement the name of Covenant, and it was the first formulation of the principles of Israelite religion, and hence of our own faith. On the other hand, there was little about personal religion in the Covenant of Moses. The laws he formed were laws of tribal morality, and the guidance of God was for the nation rather than for the individual.

Not for many generations shall we find much stress upon personal faith in a personal God.

So the wilderness trek lasted on through a whole generation. Moses's work finished when he sent out the scouts to explore the land of Canaan, to the borders of which they had come. The report, at least of two of them—Joshua and Caleb—showed that God had certainly kept to His part of the Covenant agreement, even if the course of the people had been marked by continual defections and if Moses had spent most of his life in settling disputes and arguing against people who maintained that it would have been better had they stayed to die in slavery in Egypt. Moses chose for his successor one of these scouts, who stands out as a military leader and strategist of more than ordinary capability and a man of absolute if simple faith in God. With that Moses, old now and weary of the struggle, climbed Mount Pisgah to look over the Plains of Jericho into the new land which was the end of their wanderings—and died there. So passed one of the great leaders of all time. It was a true instinct which led the later Hebrews to look back to him as the true founder of their religion and the genius who first united the loose collection of Israelite tribesmen by the secure bond of religion.

Other Semitic tribes made inroads into Canaan about the same period as these tribesmen came from Egypt. Some of these tribes were connected with Israel, being descended from Lot; but in the meantime their traditions had been fostered in other surroundings than those of the Hebrews, and history shows that a number of semi-nomad tribes were seeking to settle down to agricultural pursuits in a new land within the space of the same few generations. In this stage the religion of the Israelites, with whom we are mainly concerned, was to assume a new form. The days of the desert were behind them, and these were days of war and skirmish. The settlement in the new land was not accomplished without much bloodshed, and the belief naturally grew that the victories which did undoubtedly come to the Israelites were the victories of their God. In their thought, Jehovah became a war-Lord, and the Ark became the recognized symbol of His presence on the battlefield, so that when they failed to take it with them they almost expected defeat. In the first chapter of the Book which bears his name— though it was not written by him—Joshua is shown to have understood that he was divinely commanded to be courageous in leadership. 'Be strong and of a good courage; be not affrighted, neither be thou dismayed; for the Lord thy God is with thee whithersoever thou goest.' Jehovah Sebaoth (Hebrew for 'Lord of armies') became a proper name for God; and tribal warfare became a divine commission. Even the splendid passage in which Joshua sets before his people the choice between Jehovah and the other gods of the tribes round about (Chapter 24) is full of military imagery. He argues that they must be true to Jehovah because He is the God who has subdued their enemies.

Nevertheless, this stage of religion shows still the belief that God ordered natural phenomena to help His people. Joshua gathered his men together and they crossed the River Jordan, not by one of the two fords near the city, but as the result of a landslide which for a time dammed the river—an event which has occurred within more recent times as the result of a heavy fall of rock from the hills. Jericho was the natural objective of the Joseph tribes as they entered from this point; and here again the story is of divine intervention on their behalf through perfectly natural occurrence. An earthquake assisted the tribesmen in their siege of the city perhaps; or possibly the military stratagem which Joshua employed of a sudden blast of rams' horns—the usual rallying-sound for an army —caused a panic among the citizens. The excavations of Professor Garstang have revealed that part of the wall of Jericho was undermined (presumably by earthquake) in such a way as to make it possible for invaders to clamber over. The evidence he discovered confirmed the account in the Tell-el-Amarna letters of a powerful invasion of Palestine by Hebrews about 1400 B.C. The inhabitants surrendered either because of the earthquake or because they thought that the daily procession round their city presaged a larger force than they expected. But, in either case, the point of the story, so far as religious history is concerned, is that the victory was considered to be the result of the Ark of God being carried round in procession by the priests. For the same reason that God was Lord of warfare, it was more than criminal, it was irreligious to touch the sacred spoil of battle, as Achan learned to his cost when he looted the 'devoted thing'.

But victory did not always come to them with such ease. The story of the conquest of Palestine is told in two books in the Old Testament. Joshua seems to represent an idealized account of the greater victories; but in the Book of Judges we have an older and quite different sort of account. It tells of separate tribes waging long and sporadic warfare until, little by little, they came to possess the greater part of the land. These stories are some of the oldest literary compilations of the Bible. The Song of Deborah in Chapter 5 probably represents the earliest extant example of Hebrew poetry. The heroes of the book are called Judges, but they exercised no judicial function. They were simply and solely warriors who led their tribes to successful battle with enemy tribes at various times—men like Gideon, who felt the call of God as he skulked in the winepress to thresh his wheat, instead of doing it on the high, open ground above his farm where the wind would blow away the chaff as he beat it with his primitive flail; and whose yeoman army was reduced so drastically by the expedient of testing at the water's edge whether men were fonder of their drink than of holding their weapons fast. In some of the stories the exaggerating hand of tradition and the influence of legend have been at work, more particularly in the Samson narratives; but the Hebrew of later days saw the guiding hand of the 'Lord of armies' both in the clever device of Gideon in equipping all his men (instead of the leaders only) with trumpets and torches and thus surprising the enemy, and the superlative strength of Samson led out as a blinded captive for the sport of the people of Gaza. Eventually, however, the Joseph tribes achieved supremacy over all but the Philistines, and their chieftains or judges became for a time at least the recognized governors in the new agricultural order.

Now these nomads had never before performed agricultural tasks. How were they to know that their God, Jehovah, knew anything of growing crops? He might be very useful and competent in war, but could He produce corn? The tribes with whom they were gradually amalgamating had deities of their own, 'baals' as they called them, who they thought were responsible for each field and each natural means of growth. It was the most natural thing in the world for simple people to pay allegiance to these baals as the cause of their prosperity. They worshipped Jehovah primarily, but the shrines at which they did so were often shrines at which the fertility gods were worshipped as well. We find Samuel growing up with Eli at one of these mixed shrines at Shiloh. Obviously this impure, combined worship led to abuse.

Once again, however, God seems to have raised up a leader. Samuel grew up with the evils of the corrupt priesthood of Hophni and Phinehas as very real examples

to him, and the story of his call by God to purify the
religion of Israel leads us to see in his ministry at Ramah
the survival of the essential elements in the real religion
of Israel. He exercised a control over the excesses of the
people which makes him the link between the ancient
judges and the future kings. The interesting fact for our
purpose is that in his case, as in that of every other leader
in Israel, it was religion which made him what he was
and which gave him his sway over the people he came to
rule. With him we mark the end of another stage of
development of belief in God, for we see that the people
were learning, gradually and imperfectly, the fact that
God is Lord and Governor of every part of human life.

References

Moses—Exodus 1^1–5^{23}, 8^1–11^{10}.
The Wilderness Wanderings:
    The Passover—Exodus 12^{1-42}, Deuteronomy 16^{1-8}.
    The Red Sea—Exodus 14^1–15^{18}.
    Adventures in the desert—Exodus 15^{22}–17^{16}.
    The Covenant at Sinai—Exodus 24^{12-18}, 32^{1-26}, 20^{1-17},
        40^{1-16}.
The Scouts—Numbers 13^1–14^{45}.
Death of Moses—Deuteronomy 3^{25-9}, 34^{1-12}.
Joshua—Joshua 1^{1-9}, 6^{1-27}.
The Judges:
    Gideon—Judges 6^{1-24}, 7^{1-25}.
    Samson—Judges 16^{4-31}.
Samuel—1 Samuel 1^1–3^{21}, 7^{11-17}.

Questions for Discussion

1. Criticize the value of the religion of the wilderness
    (*a*) from the point of view of its own age, (*b*) as
    a stage in the growing idea of religion in Israel.

2. Were the later Hebrews right in regarding Moses as the greatest religious leader of their race? What limitations can you discover in his idea of God?

3. Do you feel that the stories of Joshua and the Judges are an anti-climax after the work of Moses for religion?

4. How far is it true that the Israelites when they settled in Canaan showed themselves markedly more developed than the tribesmen into whose land they had come?

5. What facts about the idea of God can be learned from the story of Eli at Shiloh? What authority do you think he had in ancient Israel?

CHAPTER FOUR

The Rise of the Kings

WE HAVE seen that the tribesmen were not unsuccessful in their new occupation of agriculture and to some degree came to terms with 'the people of the land'. Success breeds independence. But there were strong coalitions of enemy tribes, chiefly the Philistines, who cared nothing for the moral traditions of Israel, but were interested to see that these newly-settled peoples had sheep which could be stolen, rough villages which could be pillaged (the Old Testament called them 'cities', but recent archaeological discoveries have shown that the average size of these walled villages was about ten acres!), corn which could be destroyed. No one tribe was strong enough to keep them out, so in sheer self-defence they were forced to join together. With a plan for co-operation, they went to the only man who could wield any authority over them all, Samuel. They wanted a king, someone to lead them in war, such as all the other tribes had. Would he choose a man for them?

Samuel did not greet their request with the enthusiasm they expected. It was his religious conviction that Israel was God's nation and that none but He should bear rule over it. (This idea was called *theocracy*—government by God.) So he informed them that he believed it was not God's will for them to have a king, because any petty princeling might come and exact his levies of men and goods from them, and they would be infinitely worse off. But his hand was forced, for the people demanded a king. The man he chose for the task, acting under that real religious intuition of the man who believes with all his heart that his choices are directed by the God he seeks to serve, was the tall young son of a Benjamite farmer who had been sent with a servant to search the country-side for some lost asses. Today we should not think that an Archbishop would be the most likely person to ask about strayed animals, but in early Israel God was re-garded as One interested in every aspect of His people's life. Their belief was incomplete, of course, but many years later the greatest Israelite of them all was to tell the world that God as Father is concerned about the fall of the meanest sparrow. Samuel anointed Saul with oil as a symbol of his task—a symbol which is still used when our own monarchs are reminded at their coronation cere-mony that their leadership is subject to God's overruling. But Saul did not assume 'the throne' immediately. In fact, for some time to come, there were no royal pre-rogatives to assume. The time came later when he was driving some oxen, that he first accomplished the func-tion for which he had been appointed king. Nahash the Ammonite had besieged the border town of Jabesh-gilead and threatened, with Oriental ferocity, either to butcher all the inhabitants or else put out their right eyes in token to the tribes that they were his victims. When Saul heard the news, his blood rose, and he summoned the tribesmen of Israel for their first united assault by distributing chunks of bleeding ox as a warning of what would befall the oxen of the man who did not think it worth his while to join the yeomen in the defence of their fellow tribesmen. Then, after the victory was won and the Ammonite danger was averted—and only then—was Saul proclaimed king, offi-cial leader in war. But even after that he seems to have gone on with his farming and to have left it only when one of the frequent skirmishes was imminent.

There is an interesting fact to be noted about these three stories. Each appears to start as though the author were introducing us to Saul for the first time. The reason is that the author of the Books of Samuel, like those who were responsible for the other historical books of the Old Testament, was not really an author, but an editor. He collected his stories from old records and sometimes from the abundant oral traditions which abounded. To him, such a record was sacred. It had been inspired of God; else it would not have lasted. Who was he, a mere man, to alter it, or even to discriminate between the historical accuracy of various accounts of the same incident? So he inserted all the accounts he could find in the same words as they had come to him, complete with their introductions and conclusions. In the case of the appointment of Saul, the three accounts happen to be complementary and make up together a fairly logical and apparently historical account of what actually happened. But sometimes we are given two or more accounts which contradict each other in some respects. We have already met two different accounts of the Creation. Elsewhere one account records the killing of Goliath as the work of David and another as the feat of Elhanan (1 Samuel 17$^{38-51}$, 2 Samuel 21^{19} R.V.: the A.V. says that '*the brother of* Goliath' was slain by Elhanan, printing the three extra words in italics, which indicates that—as the R.V. correctly records—they did not appear in the Hebrew original). Most scholars think the same reason lies behind the fact that Mark and Matthew tell of Jesus feeding 5,000 at one time and 4,000 at another.

All through Saul's 'reign' Samuel appears to be the leading figure in the life of the people. He, not Saul, directs the policy of the race, because he is regarded as the religious authority, and for the Hebrew of this generation all life is religious. The people really thought that they were the Chosen Race and that they were settling in the Promised Land as a divinely governed nation.

D

Their battles were God's battles. The ultimate end was
assured victory, because they were not establishing their
own supremacy but vindicating Jehovah in the sight of
the enemy tribesmen. Saul is regarded by the author of
1 Samuel as the means whereby God brought about that
victory. Thus in Chapter 15 Samuel's wrath was aroused
against Saul because he regarded his conquest of the
Amalekites as a personal victory and not part of the
divine plan. Saul's instructions had been to put to death
everything which belonged to the enemy. It was all to
be 'devoted', sacrificed to God. Saul kept back part of
the spoil—sheep, oxen, and the martial leader Agag. To
Samuel, that was sacrilege. Saul had appropriated what
rightly belonged to God. So Samuel, speaking—as he
believed—for God, informed Saul that his days as king
were numbered. Such a leader was no king for Israel,
for Israel was God's people. There was no place for a
man who disobeyed or who sought his own advantage.
And, to make a visual demonstration of his belief, Samuel
'hewed Agag in pieces before the Lord'. To us, such an
act would be looked upon as cold-blooded murder; but
to a man of Samuel's primitive ideas it was a religious
act, something he did as a sign that he at least regarded
the spoil of battle as the right of the God in whose name
he believed they had won the battle. So Saul's last years
were lived under a cloud. Samuel was a disappointed
old man. He had always doubted the wisdom of monarchy. He had warned the people of what degradation
and 'irreligion' might follow—for irreligion it was to him
that any man should dare to assume that Israel belonged
to any but God. He lived to see his saddest suspicions
fulfilled. So 'Samuel came no more to see Saul until the
day of his death; for Samuel mourned for Saul: and the
Lord repented that He had made Saul king over Israel'.

The early historian cleverly draws the picture of Saul

as an old man growing short-tempered and autocratic as a result of his selfish rejection of God's primacy. Once he had been able to tell a story about the Battle of Michmash, when Saul swore a mighty oath that his warriors should vanquish the Philistines before any man should have a meal; and of his righteous indignation when he discovered that his own son, Jonathan, had broken the 'taboo' through ignorance that the vow had been made. He was quite prepared to keep his pledged word and let his son be sacrificed because it was an oath made to God, but the people intervened and said that one who had secured such victory for them should be spared in any case. But at the end of his tale, the chronicler has to tell of an old man, fiery in temper, who has to be appeased with music when melancholia overtakes him, and who plots to secure the death of one whom he has come to see as a rival in the popular choice of the people. (Even his disease is attributed to the departure of the Spirit of the Lord from him.) Just at the very last the writer shows us the brave warrior at the Battle of Mount Gilboa, prepared to fall on his own sword rather than to be the victim of his pagan enemies.

The young rival was, of course, David. Once again he is introduced to us in two independent stories. In one he is the young farmer's son who charms Saul's fits by his skill on the harp. In the other, he is the fearless young brave who faces and defeats Goliath; not, be it noted, in virtue of his great skill or powerful arm, but because he attacked his great adversary 'in the name of the Lord of hosts, the God of the armies of Israel'. For one reason or the other, David joined Saul's court and rose in esteem by leaps and bounds, until the women were singing that—

Saul hath slain his thousands,
And David his ten thousands.

That created jealousy between the two, and only the loyalty of his wife Michal, the daughter of Saul, and of his friend Jonathan, Saul's son, saved David from death. David spent the next few years as leader of a band of outlaws. He was the Hebrew Robin Hood, who gathered round him a crowd of rough malcontents and, having won their allegiance by the nobility of his own character, made them into a band who used their strength to protect the scattered border farmers from the ravages of sheep-stealers from neighbouring tribes. There was nothing very moral or even legal about the position of David and his men in this time, but at least the virtues of loyalty and bravery are shown in their attitude. To our modern view of religion and morality, there is not much to be said in favour of David's behaviour toward Nabal (1 Samuel 25), though we find much to honour in the David who rejected the water from the well at Bethlehem for which he longed, but which had been brought to him at the risk of men's lives (2 Samuel 23$^{14-17}$), and in the man who more than once spared the life of his enemy, Saul, when he had a chance to take him unbeknown.

When Saul died by his own hand, it was to David that the people turned for leadership first of the northern part of the country, and later of the united tribes. In his reign we see a notable advance in religion and statesmanship. So prominent is this fact that the later historians all looked back to the age of David as a golden age of their story; and when after the Exile the nation came to have glad anticipations of one who, appointed by God, should lead the people to prosperity and peace again as king indeed (i.e. the Messiah), it was to the family of David that they looked for the expected hero. None but David could be the forefather of the ideal king of the future. The fact was that David combined in his own person skill in government, prowess in battle, abundant common sense, a great love for his fellow men, a power of evoking their allegiance in all difficulties, and above all a sense of devotion to God as he knew Him and a passionate desire to work out His will in the national life. Samuel told Saul that David was a man after God's own heart. He had all the religious instinct of Samuel combined with much more practical ability to unite the tribes. He was the kind of man who would search out Mephibosheth, the lame son of his old friend Jonathan. 'Is there not yet any of the house of Saul,' he asked, 'that I may show the kindness of God unto him?' The great stain upon his character was his sin in putting Uriah the Hittite in a vulnerable position in battle and then marrying his widow, Bathsheba. The historians did not condemn him for this, as we should, for all else in his life gives us the impression of a man who was just in every respect. But Nathan's parable of the man with one ewe lamb and David's penitence constitute one of the noblest stories in the Old Testament, and show the ethical and religious object of the whole history. David spent so much time in deciding the petty issues between man and man that, when his son Absalom wanted to win the loyalty of the people from his father, the only way he could do it was to assume the position of judge where his father was unable to do so through pressure of work.

David's reign was one long war with various tribes-men. Part of it was spent in ignoble strife with the remnants of Saul's followers, and some, much against his will, with his own son who rebelled against him. The son was killed only by the treachery of the commander-in-chief who acted in direct contravention of David's orders, and by so doing drew from David the cry of lament which has become so famous—'O my son Absalom, my son, my son Absalom! Would God I had died for thee, O Absalom, my son, my son!' The lament is remembered when the name of Joab is forgotten; just as the battles against the Philistines are not recorded in detail.

But it is as a man of religion that David is always remembered. He is linked for ever with Jerusalem. When the tribesmen came together to beg him to become king of the whole race, he 'spotted' the hill Zion which he thought to be impregnable, and there he established his primitive capital. Strategically, it was an excellent choice. Religiously, it was a stroke of inspired genius. To Jerusalem David brought the Ark of the Covenant—the box which held the sacred relics to remind men of the guidance of God during the wilderness wanderings. There in visible form the people had a permanent memorial of the God who ruled their nation. If they were to be a nation, God was to be King and Lord. With the connivance and assistance of Nathan, the prophet, David first laid the plans to build a Temple there in Jerusalem, which should be the centre of the worship of Jehovah for the whole nation. This was a great step forward. It meant that the day was past when God was regarded as one of a number of deities, who should be worshipped side by side with the gods of wind and rain and field and tree—the baals of the people of the land. Later, it is true, a reaction set in and Elijah came to feel that he alone was left in Israel as a true Jehovah worshipper, but David first marks the stage when the Hebrews passed from the worship of many gods. The court chroniclers he established were to record for future ages the progress of state and religion, and to them we owe the records which were consulted by the later compilers of our Bible. To their brilliant contemporary account we owe our vivid picture of the history of David's reign.

But, when all is said, it remains to be added that David's religion was that of his age and not of ours. He acted as though he realized that the kingship of the chosen race put him in a position as God's representative, but when the Ark was brought to Jerusalem we are told that 'he danced before the Lord with all his might'—not a very inspiring, nor necessarily a very religious spectacle to our ideas. But the people of his day interpreted his action as that of a genuine man, who was serving his God according to his lights. If he was a warrior primarily, his interest in the new sanctuary at Jerusalem was honest enough. Men like Nathan could rebuke him in the name of the Lord (as in the parable of the one ewe lamb) and still maintain his friendship and respect. His faith was the faith of his age at its highest, and in that sense he was infinitely superior to Saul and to Solomon and his successors. That he was religious, according to the ideas of his time, and that he was exceptional in that respect, is demonstrated by the fact that later ages looked upon the Psalms as typical of his religious experience. The records told that his fame as a musician had spread far and wide, and his poetic ability is evidenced by his lament over Jonathan and Saul (2 Samuel 1^{17-27}). The Psalm style of writing may easily date from his age. When other ages adopted the form of composition which he may have made popular, and incorporated in it many later and nobler ideas of God—ideas derived from the great prophets and reflecting the later history and more advanced discovery of the ways of God with His people— they paid tribute to David's memory by connecting his name with the whole of this form of religious literature. But the whole Book of Psalms must be considered later.

He was eventually succeeded by his son Solomon, who was designated to the throne by his father at the instigation of his mother, Bathsheba, and Nathan the prophet. He was a statesman and made it his task to establish Israel as one of the nations of the ancient world. There are records in the histories of those days which show that the amalgam of tribes was at last regarded as a nation. Solomon ruled over more territory than his father had done; he established trade relationships with Hiram, the Phoenician king; the Queen of Sheba visited him officially, because he was famous in the ancient world for his practical wisdom. The olive oil of Palestine was traded for necessary goods. Court officials came into being. Above all, the Temple planned by David was built—a magnificent affair, reflecting the prosperity of the age, though it was primarily a chapel royal, attached to the more splendid palace.

We need to remind ourselves that the Temple was very different from anything we know. It was an open court for the most part, totally unlike our conception of a cathedral. There was an altar, but it was the least ornate part of the building, and around it stood the priests with their great knives ready to kill the beasts of all sorts which were brought by the worshippers. The idea of sacrifice was very old, dating from the first recognition that God had given all growing things to man for his subsistence. Men felt quite rightly that the first product of the farm— the earliest wine, the first calf or lamb to be born, and so on—properly belonged to God. The only means of presenting them to God was by sacrifice; and the worship of the splendid Temple consisted almost entirely of the butchering of hundreds of beasts. There was nothing comparable at this time with our hymn-singing, reading of the Scriptures (for there were as yet none to read; the first books of our Old Testament were not to be written for many years yet), or preaching, and almost the sole function of the priests was to maintain the daily sacrifice in the sacred place.

Such an edifice cost a great deal, and taxation was high. Solomon forced his people to work upon his Temple, and upon the palace he built for himself. He was an autocrat, and his people hated him. The Temple had been planned as a tribute to the God who had delivered His people, but it was always known as Solomon's Temple, not as Jehovah's. That was the main trouble. The redeeming feature of the whole process is reflected in the deep sense of reverence which is apparent when Solomon made his speech at the dedication of the Temple (2 Chronicles 6[12-42]). 'But will God in very deed dwell on the earth?' he asked. 'Behold, heaven and the heaven of heavens cannot contain Thee; how much less this house which I have builded?" Was that all a pose—an assumed piety put on for the occasion? We hope not. All we can say is that the historian gives us the idea that Solomon glorified himself and exacted respect for Israel from the nations very much more than he advanced the true love of God. In spite of all the gold and precious things, the sacrifices seem to have meant less to the people than in David's day. It was an age of tremendous national progress, but its main interest for the Hebrew historian is that succeeding generations should learn from it that formality does not necessarily mean sincerity.

Solomon was not merely an ostentatious, extravagant tyrant; he was a man of great common sense, which brought him almost as much fame as his Temple. Someone must have collected some of his 'wise sayings', and these may have formed the basis (but only the basis; just as David's compilations may have formed the basis of the Book of Psalms) of the book in our Bible known as Proverbs. (The title word translated 'Proverbs' would be better rendered as 'Wise Sayings'.) But, like so many very clever people, Solomon was not quite clever enough. His latter years show him to have been led away by the various religious beliefs of the multitude of his foreign wives; and, with the decay of his vital belief in Jehovah and the growing hatred of his oppressive rule, the Edomite

tribes to the East became independent again. The process of disintegration of the nation had set in already, and
was soon to be carried a great deal further. To the ancient
historian, the reason is obvious. God had been usurped
by man.

The further stage came immediately after his death,
when his bumptious son, Rehoboam, went to receive the
allegiance of the people, which he quite thought was his
by right, though no theory of succession had yet been
evolved. The people wanted to know whether the bad
rule of his tyrannical father was to be continued; and
when he rather foolishly followed the advice of the young
men rather than that of the sage old counsellors, and said
that his little finger would be thicker than his father's
loins, there arose from the back of the crowd a revolutionary adventurer who had been exiled, and who yelled
the rebel shout, 'To your tents, O Israel.' Jeroboam, for
that was his name, became ruler of ten of the tribes in
the north, and Rehoboam was left with the two southern
tribes and the ancient capital at Jerusalem. From now
on we have to follow the fortunes of two kingdoms. Thus
early have the tribesmen split up again. But there was
much more to it than a revolt about royal succession.
Jeroboam saw that, if his people were to go to Jerusalem
to worship in Solomon's Temple, his rival would have
an admirable opportunity of corrupting their loyalty and
persuading them to rejoin his standard. So Jeroboam hit
upon the plan of setting up rival shrines at Bethel and
Dan in his kingdom, where Jehovah was worshipped in
the form of a bull. The people accepted his explanation
that these shrines were just as good, and were to save
them the trouble of trekking to Jerusalem. It is not difficult to imagine what result this move would have. If
God could be worshipped in the form of a bull, He was
very different in significance to the people from the God

we know. Such a God could soon become regarded again as one of the gods of the nations, and the progress of religion—God's revelation of His will and purpose—would be put back 300 years. That is precisely what did happen.

If things were bad in the northern kingdom, they were little better in the south. Rehoboam was weak. Sheshonk of Egypt invaded his country and subdued him, and that started the long period of Egyptian domination of Palestine.

There was only one escape from this situation if Israel was to continue her development as the people to whom God had entrusted the revelation of His nature to the world. God would have to make some new form of appeal. The revelation in history had done a certain amount, but it was not enough. Men needed to hear a voice of enthusiasm, which should recall them to their faith in the divine order of the universe and of their national hopes. Thus are we introduced to the first form of real prophecy.

References

The Choice of a King—1 Samuel 8[4-22], 9[1-24], 10[1-9], 11[1-13].

Exploits of Saul and Jonathan—1 Samuel 13[1]-14[46].

The Coming of David—1 Samuel 16[14-23], 17[1-58].

Saul's Jealousy and Jonathan's Friendship—1 Samuel 18[1-16], 19[1-17], 20[1-42].

David the Outlaw—1 Samuel 21[1-9], 26[1-25], 2 Samuel 23[8-17].

Saul's death; David becomes king—1 Samuel 31[1-13]; 2 Samuel 1[17-27], 2[1-7], 3[1], 5[4-12], 6[1-15].

David as King—2 Samuel 7[1-11], 9[1-13], 11[1-12, 15], 15[1-6], 18[1-33].

Solomon—1 Kings 4[21-34], 5[1-18], 6[1-10], 8[12-56], 10[1-13], 11[9-13, 26].

The Division of the Kingdom—1 Kings 12[1-20, 25-33].

Questions for Discussion

1. How far do you agree with Samuel that monarchy was a national evil?
2. What did Israel owe to Saul?
3. Why do we use David and Jonathan as examples of friendship?
4. What moral virtues have we learned since David's day?
5. Make a list of the reasons why David was regarded as the ideal king.
6. Do you think Solomon was a victim of his own ambition?
7. Was the building of Solomon's Temple more important as a political or as a religious move?
8. Did the people gain or lose by the disruption of the monarchy?

CHAPTER FIVE

The Prophets and the Nation

JEROBOAM'S action in setting up the bulls at Dan and Bethel was in all probability not quite so much of a pagan reaction as we are apt to imagine. The bull, the strongest animal the Canaanites knew, was often used as a symbol of the strength of Jehovah, even in the Temple at Jerusalem and perhaps on the very Ark itself. But the later historians regarded it as the final apostasy which marred all the future progress of the race. The author of the Books of Kings never tired of referring in disparaging terms to the evil influence of the 'sin wherewith Jeroboam, the son of Nebat, made Israel to sin'. He records of each king that he 'did that which was evil [or "that which was right"] in the sight of the Lord', and these phrases represent his judgement as to whether the king did or did not support the bull-worship of Jeroboam. A king who 'did that which was right' was not necessarily a good ruler, but one who turned his back on the worship of the shrines. Jeroboam's real error was in encouraging the continuation of old customs which, though they may have been good enough in the past, were demoralizing to a developing people and held back the advancement of the knowledge of God.

To the historian it only meant one thing. A nation which has corrupted its religion will have a corrupt history. He could illustrate that fact easily. The years from 937 until about 860 B.C. were marked by an unworthy conflict between Israel, the northern province, and Judah, the southern kingdom. That was divine retribution, the author considered. But so was the rise of the great war-lords of Damascus, the Syrian kings, Tabrimmon and Ben-hadad, who forced their attentions on the northern kingdom in no small measure. The last-mentioned, in fact, overran the northern outposts in Galilee. Israel was unfortunate in having a succession of weak and inefficient rulers, but that only proved the editor's point.

When Omri eventually succeeded to the throne in Israel (for we must leave the varying fortunes of the southern kingdom for a while), he proved to be all that his predecessors had not been. He was an energetic warrior who did more for his country than any before him. He kept back the Syrians under Ben-hadad; and, though from the Syrian records we can see that he had to suffer many setbacks, he had the cause of his nation at heart. He was one of the greatest of the northern kings, yet the Bible historian dismisses his reign in a few short verses (1 Kings 16²¹⁻⁸) and says nothing of his political moves or of his campaigns. Why? Simply because he was not a religious man. He took very little interest one way or another in the worship of Jehovah or of the baals, and so the historian has nothing to say about him. According to his ideas, Omri's reign should have been one of defeat and ignominy as a retribution for his irreligion. As things did not turn out that way, he glosses over his reign quickly, for it was after all a history of religion that he had set out to write.

His son, Ahab, receives much more attention, chiefly because of his open revolt against the religion of his fathers. Politically he continued his father's policy. But the main interest in his reign comes through marriage with Jezebel, the Sidonian princess. Omri had arranged this marriage as an astute move to bring his nation into alliance with that of Ethbaal of Phoenicia. Jezebel brought with her the worship of the baal of her country, Melkart.

Ahab, like Solomon before him, found place for his wife's religion in the court; and it was not long before the tolerant syncretism (alliance of the religion of Jehovah with the cult of the baals, as at the local shrines) gave way to a thoroughgoing form of paganism.

This was the situation which gave rise to the most picturesque figure we have yet found in the Old Testament —Elijah. He was a Jehovah fanatic, wild and unkempt. He believed that Israel's abandonment of the old shepherd way of life and adoption of the new agricultural habits was the real cause of all her ills. To him civilization and statecraft, with their accompaniments of towns and buildings and officials, were all of the devil. Yet this strange dervish had a peculiar fascination both for the people and the king. He summoned the king and the officials of the baal worship to a demonstration on Mount Carmel, away from the wicked cities, and with impassioned oratory demanded how long the nation was to 'limp on the two knee-joints'. If Jehovah was to be the Lord of Israel, then He should be worshipped; but if the baals were to be the national deities, let them prove their worth in the affairs of the nation. Not only the lightning-flash, igniting the prepared altar, but Elijah's whole enthusiasm and sincerity led the people to declare their fundamental loyalty to the religion of the preceding generations. The whole challenge of the Carmel story was accentuated by the drought and consequent famine of the time. The baals had failed to produce crops. Elijah's God sent the rain which spelled prosperity. Hence the prophet's anxiety to know of the cloud, 'as small as a man's hand', and his excitement as he ran before Ahab's chariot to Jezreel (1 Kings 18[41-6]).

Such reformation as there was on the part of Ahab was short-lived, however, for we next find him in a fit of melancholy because Naboth would not surrender his vineyard at the king's pleasure. Two points of interest strike us in this story. In the first place, we are shown a state of monarchy where the king had not yet achieved complete power over his people: Naboth could refuse to sell his vineyard if he chose. The second fact is that there must have been some strong reason for Naboth to refuse so tempting an offer of a better vineyard. He declared that it was a family heritage; but he meant by that assertion that Jehovah had been worshipped on that piece of ground for generations. In the primitive belief of his time, if his vineyard passed over to the possession of one who worshipped Melkart, it would become the property of the baal and cease to incur the blessing of Jehovah. This is an instance of the idea that one god ruled one part of the world, whilst other parts belonged to the sway of other gods. The correct name for this stage of religion next above polytheism is henotheism—the veneration of one particular deity without the denial that other gods may exist.

Jezebel found a method of getting rid of Naboth, and with great skill the Hebrew historian shows to what immoral lengths the followers of the baals would go to achieve their ends. In this he was right. There was always the moral background to the true religion of Jehovah which was lacking in the faith of the people of the land. Elijah, in spite of his bold approach to Ahab, lived in fear of his life. He complained that he was alone in his loyalty to Jehovah, and that they sought his life, as indeed Jezebel did. She had vowed to make his life as the life of the baal prophets he had killed after Carmel. He was not alone, as it turned out, for there were 7,000 who had not bowed the knee to baal; and the mission he fulfilled was more than anything else responsible for the growing discontent against the house of Omri which found later expression in the bloody revolution of Jehu (2 Kings 9).

How were these quaint dervishes like Elijah received by their contemporaries? They certainly had an authority both over the people and the king. They were 'holy men'—men whose whole lives were devoted to the service of their God. Many of the pictures we have of Elijah and Elisha are little more elevating than that of the African witch-doctor; but they were sacrosanct because they were the mouthpieces of the divine. So, when they spoke, it was not merely a promulgation of Elijah or another, but it was the very Word of God. They did not prefix their remarks with the statement, 'As far as I can see . . .', but with 'Thus saith the Lord'.

By the time the old man Elijah was at the end of his days, he had a band of followers, one of whom, Elisha, was chosen to be his successor. The end of one man's mission and the beginning of the next is portrayed in dramatic form. They went together on a circuit of the villages, and at each village the inhabitants could see that Elijah was not long for this world. 'Knowest thou that the Lord will take away thy master from thy head today?' The end came in the vividness of a tropical storm. The streaking lightning in the sky appeared to Elisha as the 'chariots of Israel and the horsemen thereof'. At length Elijah disappeared, and Elisha assumed his mantle and staff, and with them his position in Israel. The stories we have of him are strikingly similar to those of Elijah (compare the story of the widow of Zarephath and her son in 1 Kings 17^8-24 with the story of the Shunammite woman in 2 Kings 4^8-37), but there are differences. The way in which Naaman the Syrian came to a prophet in a country with which his race was at war shows that Elisha transcended the nationalism with which Elijah's work was marked. Elijah was associated with the natural and supernatural phenomena of drought and storm, whilst Elisha moved among men as a healer and adviser, not

E

exclaiming so often against evil as his predecessor had done, but using the subtleties of diplomacy to accomplish his ends. If Elisha had more to show for his life's work, it is Elijah who is remembered as the representative of God in an evil age, and who was regarded in New Testament times as immortal (see Matthew 17[10-12]).

But we get another insight into the meaning of prophecy by another story from Ahab's reign (1 Kings 22[1-40]). After many years of antagonism, Israel and Judah were forced to join against the preponderant strength of the Syrian invaders. Jehoshaphat of Judah was an enlightened and accomplished ruler, and he agreed to Ahab's plan for a coalition at the Battle of Ramoth-gilead. As usual before a battle, the prophets were called in to advise the kings as to the chances of success. This was not because the prophets could foresee the result. That was not their function. They were not men gifted with second sight; but they were the political as well as the religious advisers of the time. In this case, one prophet stood out uncompromising and alone, as Elijah had been. Micaiah-ben-Imlah alone believed that disaster would follow the attack, and for his pains in saying so Ahab put him in jail. Now here was a serious religious problem. Other men, equally professing to be prophets inspired of God, said that victory would accompany the united armies. How could both be right? The writer of Kings suggests that God Himself had misled them by 'a lying spirit' which He put in their mouths—an idea particularly repellent to Christian people. So there were true prophets and false prophets; and the only means of telling whether a prophet was true or false was by the test Jesus suggested long after—'By their fruits shall ye know them'. The men who stand out in the Old Testament were men whose prophecies were vindicated by events. They did not generally foretell the distant future, but, because of their receptivity to divine revelation, they had insight into the likely outcome of immediate events. They did not advise only the individual in his moral and spiritual quest, for this was still the age of national religion, but they did play an increasingly important part in the affairs of Israel as a nation. Through them, God sometimes shaped history. Religion is that which includes the whole of life, but the age of personal religion is not yet. Men felt their way towards God who cares for the individual by coming to understand the concern of God for the nation.

This is, politically speaking, one of the periods of Israel's history when she reached honour and fame among the people of the ancient world. The most important military event of Ahab's reign goes unmentioned in Kings, because it had no religious significance. According to the Black Obelisk (now in the British Museum), which records his victories, Shalmaneser III of Assyria went to attack the northern state of Hamath and was met by a strong coalition of Syrian and Palestinian tribesmen, of whom Ahab of Israel contributed nearly as many men and more chariots than Ben-hadad of Syria. This information, too, gives us the first firmly established date in Israelite history, for this Battle of Karkar was fought in 853 B.C. At this time, then, Israel counted for something in the politics of the East.

But we are anticipating. The Battle of Ramoth-gilead to which we referred a moment ago brought the reign of Ahab to an end. He, disguised as a peasant, was pierced by an arrow show by a soldier who 'drew his bow at a venture', and had died by the time his men brought him to his city of Jezreel. It seems from the strange story in 2 Kings 9 that Elisha was responsible for stirring up a court revolution, as the result of which an outlaw adventurer, Jehu, seized the throne. It is not the choice we should have expected of a religious enthusiast like Elisha,

but this is an excellent example of the way in which the
prophets, with the conception of their divinely appointed
office, acted in politics as well as in religion. Jehu and
his dynasty reigned in the north for a century (from the
death of Ahab in 842 to the conspiracy of Shallum in
743), during which Syria more than engaged the military attentions of the powerful Assyrians. Israel took
advantage of the opportunity, and in that century of
peace she became prosperous. In fact, 'peace' and 'prosperity' came to be almost synonymous terms in Hebrew.
By the end of the period, when Jeroboam II was king
(782–743), the nation had become accustomed to the
luxurious life, and all the usual evils followed in the
wake of wealth. The rich neglected and despised the poor,
and class distinctions became real and sordid things; morality was an inconvenience and looked upon as prudish.
As for religion, it had become respectable—the 'done
thing'—and so almost meaningless. The shrines were
never so well patronized and the sacrifices were more
ornate and expensive than ever; but it is unwise to
measure the sincerity of the congregation only by the
money in the collection plate. Was it not Jesus who
pointed out that the surreptitiously offered farthing of
the widow was more of a true offering than the gold
pieces of the rich?

It was this situation which gave rise to a new form of
prophecy. We have seen how Elijah and his dervish
friends made their mark upon the paganism of their day.
In the eighth century the problem was not out-and-out
paganism, but that more sophisticated and subtle enemy
—complacency. The cudgels were taken up by a group
of prophets who have left on record some of the virile
sermons they used to preach. They are the first 'writing'
prophets. Before we look at them individually, it will be
wise for us to know something of their ideals and their

'technique'. First, we ought to remember that prophecy was not primarily foretelling what would happen in the future. It is true that every now and again they did venture to declare what they believed would be the course of God's plan for His world in some respect, as we shall see later they did in asserting that God would raise up a promised king to lead the people: but it would be quite wrong for us to assume that the prophets thought for one moment that what they had to say would have any point or purpose for our twentieth century, or indeed for any age but their own. Even their idea of the Messiah-king was very different from the King who ultimately came. The prophets have a very real message for us today, but it is quite wrong to limit that message—as some Christians try to do—to a mysterious sort of prognostication of events of today in veiled language which has to be interpreted. It is useless, for example, to try to find any 'forecast' of the rise of Hitler or the discovery of atomic energy. The Bible is a book which reveals God, but God is not revealed by that kind of thing.

No, the task of the prophets was first to preach. They were men of intense conviction about the plan they believed God to have for His people. They were quite sure that what they had to say rightly interpreted the purpose of God for the nation. With utter sincerity, they announced that they had been called of God to make proclamation of a message. 'I heard the voice of the Lord saying, Whom shall I send?' said one of them (Isaiah 6[8]), and another, Amos, said that the prophet could no more restrain his message than a man could restrain his fear when he heard the lion roar (Amos 3[8]). Jeremiah, almost despairing of his lack of success as a preacher, vowed that he would never speak again in the name of God; but he felt immediately as though there was 'a burning fire shut up' in his bones (Jeremiah 20[9]).

Men are quick to sense when a speaker is sincere and is uttering something more than a mere expression of his own views on a subject. That is partly why we give the name of 'sermon' to a particular kind of religious address which sets out, not to give the preacher a chance to expound his own pet theories, but to declare what is the revealed will of God.

The prophetic sermons are known as 'oracles' because in some sense they were the message of God through the prophets to the people. Of course, the personality of the speaker modified the form the 'oracle' took. Quite frequently it was a kind of object lesson drawn from some common fact of ordinary life, like Jeremiah's visit to the potter's shed (Chapter 18); sometimes an analogy from history, like the first two chapters of Amos. More often than not it was an energetic tirade against the people or the kings—for kings were very frequently the butts for the prophetic vehemence—and seldom did the prophet spare his words. But whatever he said was prefixed with the phrase (borrowed from the first prophets), 'Thus saith the Lord'. It was not just his opinion, but he was announcing a divine truth which had come to him; and, such is the power of moral authority, people accepted the message from the prophets as 'the Word of God'.

Not all the prophets were of a professional class, like the priests. Amos, the first we have to consider, was a shepherd in the hills at Tekoa in the south; and he made it very clear that he was not a prophet from choice, but from an urgent sense of divine call. 'I was no prophet', he declared, 'neither was I a prophet's son . . . but the Lord took me from following the flock . . . and said . . . Go, prophesy unto My people, Israel.' He was no orator of fine words and polished phrases. He saw what wealth had done to the people in the north, and he proclaimed with brutal directness what was wrong with their lives.

'Things have come to such a pass that an Israelite will
sell another into slavery because he is unable to pay a
debt of the price of a pair of sandals. As for legal justice,
when the poor widow comes to get redress in the local
court of the elders of the village which meets in the gate
at evening, it is a mere travesty. Oh, I know your outward religious observances are kept up; but even if you
sacrifice every morning instead of once a year and bring
the tenth part of your produce as a thanksgiving to God
not once every three years as the Law demands, but every
three days, that will not secure your membership of the
family of God. As a matter of fact, you get quite a religious thrill out of your new rites, and that is your reward.
Don't you understand? You are God's own people, you
think you are the only nation in human history which
has been directly guided by God through the generations
(such was Israel's exclusiveness!); and for that very cause
God will expect a higher standard from you. God is
just, so "let judgement roll down like waters and righteousness as a mighty stream". You are looking forward to a
"day of the Lord", when you think God will vindicate
your nation in the eyes of all men. Take care that such
a day does not overtake you and turn out to be a day of
judgement for you rather than for the people you think
have oppressed you—a day of darkness and not light'
(Amos 2^6, 5^{12}, 4^{4-6}, 3^2, 5^{24}, 5^{20}).

We have no record of what reception the plutocrats of
750 B.C. accorded this kind of address, as they lay on
their 'silken cushions' and gorged themselves on expensive foods and decorated themselves with the costliest
cosmetics (Amos 6^{4-6}). But what is important for us is
that in the eighth century before Jesus came one seer at
least had learned that God made moral demands of men
because He acted in a moral way towards them. From
the basis of the justice of God, which Amos first clearly

enunciated, Jesus came to assert that 'if thou art offering thy gift at the altar, and there rememberest that thy brother hath aught against thee, leave there thy gift before the altar, and go thy way, first be reconciled to thy brother, and then come and offer thy gift' (Matthew 5²³⁻⁴).

Hosea approached the same problem in a different way. He, too, realized the grim truth that Israel had been spoiled by prosperity. Some of his oracles may date from a few years after the death of Jeroboam II and reflect the age of worthless usurpers who had no concern but for their own ends. The prophet's own life was shadowed by the greatest tragedy a man can know—his wife had proved disloyal to him, and no advances which his love for her could make would secure her return to him. She was a thoroughly evil woman. Then the prophet realized how illustrative this was of God's relations with His people. God had been guiding the history of the race from earliest times. He it was who had brought them from Egypt and enabled them to settle in Palestine (11¹), and even given them their Law (4⁶), their sacrificial system (8¹³), their prophets (6⁵), and their monarchy. Yet when they came in contact with other tribesmen, they promptly ignored that record of providential guidance and proved disloyal to Jehovah. If Hosea's wife spent her time with other men, Israel neglected Jehovah in favour of the baals. It was the same plaint as had called forth Amos's insistence upon the justice of God, but to Hosea the situation indicated the supreme *love* of God which was not destroyed even by Israel's unfaithfulness and disloyalty. So the prophet tried to woo back Israel to faith in Jehovah and to sincerity of worship. 'O Israel, return unto the Lord thy God' (14¹), who has loved you even from the days of Egypt. To Hosea, God was no longer the distant deity who could only be approached through the

magnificence of a temple like Solomon's, but One, the greatness of whose love revealed the unique relation in which
Israel stood to Him. It was because 'there is no truth,
nor mercy, nor knowledge of God in the land. There is
nought but making and breaking oaths, and killing, and
stealing', that 'the Lord hath a controversy with the
inhabitants of the land' (4^{1-2}). How blind Israel had
been! She had acted as though the agricultural produce
was due to the gift of the baals, little realizing that
Jehovah had given the corn and wine and olive oil which
brought prosperous trade, and even had been responsible
for the gold and silver which was mined. Instead of
accepting these gifts gratefully, Israel had used them to
adorn the baal idols and shrines. When Hosea portrayed
the character of God who loved His people in spite of all
that, he had made a great step towards the New Testament
idea of God and His nature.

For the next twenty years, the voice of the prophets
was drowned in that of political ferment. 2 Kings 15
and 17 present a swiftly moving panorama of national
catastrophe. Up in the north, Assyria had consolidated
her position and was apparently preparing to attack Israel
in order to make it a forward base for a thrust southwards
into the rich Egyptian lands. In Israel itself kings were
enthroned and as quickly murdered. Zechariah, Shallum,
Menahem—their names come in rapid succession. We
can just discern what is happening when 15^{19} informs us
briefly that Menahem had to pay annual tribute to the
great king of Assyria, Tiglath-pileser III, whom the
Hebrew historian here calls Pul. That tribute meant
heavy taxation in Israel. Then on goes the narrative again
—more intrigue, more murder. Pekahiah, Pekah, and
finally Hoshea are found on the throne of the northern
kingdom. If only the people had maintained some consistent policy of alliance with the greater power, and if only

they had seen the truth that morality, honesty, kindliness, and all that is meant by true religion so widely affects a nation in time of crisis, Israel might yet have remained as a kingdom subservient to Assyria, but nevertheless a kingdom. As it was, one faction counselled alliance with Egypt, the other submission to Assyria, and the government could not make up its mind. 'Ephraim is a silly dove, without understanding', declared Hosea (7^{11}); 'they call unto Egypt, they go to Assyria'. So the inevitable climax drew on. At last Shalmaneser V of Assyria discovered that his puppet, Hoshea of Israel, had intrigued behind his back with King So of Egypt. He marched down to his capital, Samaria, and for three years besieged it. Just before the Israelites submitted, Shalmaneser died, and his successor, Sargon II, claims the victory: 'In the beginning of my reign [722] . . . Samaria I besieged and took. . . . 27,290 inhabitants I carried away. . . . I set up again and made more populous than before. People from lands which I had taken I settled there. My men I set over them as governors.' It is a sordid story of an obstinate race. We wonder whether Amos and Hosea lived to see the ruin of the nation they had tried desperately, but by such different methods, to save.

References

Omri and Ahab—1 Kings 16^{15-34}.
Micaiah and Ahab—1 Kings 22^{1-40}.
Elijah—1 Kings 17^{1}–19^{16}, 21^{1-29}; 2 Kings 2^{1-18}.
Elisha—2 Kings 4^{1-37}, 5^{1-27}, 6^{8-23}, 7^{1-20}.
Amos 3^{1-8}, 8^{1-14}, 1^{2}–2^{16}, 6^{1-8}, 4^{1-13}, 5^{1-27}.
Hosea 4^{1-9}, 6^{1-11}, 7^{1-3}, $^{11-16}$, 11^{1-5}, 12^{1-2}, 14^{1-9}.
The downfall of Israel and sack of Samaria—2 Kings 14^{23-9}, 15^{8-31}, 17^{1-12}.

Questions for Discussion

1. From the stories of Elijah and Micaiah, estimate what force prophecy had in the days of Ahab.
2. What exactly was the victory Elijah gained on Mount Carmel? Did he regard it as a victory?
3. Does our modern Christianity owe anything to Elijah and Elisha?
4. Can you trace any parallels from other ages of the history of other races with the conditions at the time of Amos and Hosea, and with their task as reformers?
5. From hints given by Amos and Hosea make a list of the social wrongs of the eighth century B.C.
6. What is your opinion about the rightness or wrongness of the historian's summary of the causes of the downfall of Israel in 2 Kings 17$^{7-41}$?

CHAPTER SIX

The Failure of the South

AFTER the fall of Samaria in 722 B.C. the southern province was left to combat alone the invasions of Assyria and Egypt, the world empires to north and south which for hundreds of years threatened the existence of the Hebrew race. Judah, as the southern province was named, had never fallen into such moral chaos as had the north; and the pitiful tale of usurpers and revolts which, as we have seen, constituted the political history of the north, was avoided in the south because for four centuries it was ruled by a single dynasty descended from David. Also, Jerusalem was an admirable capital, rather off the main trade routes from north to south, and remained intact for many generations. After the reign of Rehoboam (where we left the fortunes of the south to concentrate our attention on the north) there was for some time war between the two states, but we have already seen (p. 58) how Jehoshaphat of Judah allied with Ahab of Israel at Ramoth-gilead. This alliance lasted for some time, and there followed a rather uninteresting period which added little to the religious development until the reign of Hezekiah, who seems to have come to the throne of Judah a few years before Samaria fell in 722. He is famous for having built a remarkable aqueduct, some of the solid stone sections of which are still visible today (pictures of these are in Frank Morison's *And Pilate Said*), which provided Jerusalem with a fresh supply of water even during siege. The Pool of Siloam of New Testament fame is really the underground basin into which the water ran (2 Kings 20[20]).

The first three chapters of the Book of Micah help us to see the situation at the outset of Hezekiah's reign. (The other chapters seem to have been copied on to the same roll, but were probably the work of a later prophet who tried to sum up what Amos, Hosea, Isaiah, and Micah himself had taught: 'Will the Lord be pleased with thousands of rams, or with ten thousands of rivers of oil? . . . He hath shewed thee, O man, what is good; and what doth the Lord require of thee, but to do justly, and to love mercy, and to walk humbly with thy God?' (6⁷⁻⁸).) Micah belonged to the country. He saw how the poor were downtrodden and robbed by wealthy landowners who could seize their humble property (2²). Such social injustice cried aloud for the vengeance of heaven, as much as did the prophets who 'make my people to err' (3⁵) and the monstrous evils of the cities of Jerusalem and Samaria (1⁵). Upon them all would fall the punishment of God.

During Hezekiah's reign came the great attack (701 B.C.) of Sennacherib, the successor of Sargon II of Assyria, preparatory to which his three ambassadors were sent to treat with their opposite numbers in Judah. The Rabshakeh (his title means 'chief cupbearer'), finding that his persuasive argument that Israel should make an alliance with Assyria was of no avail, started to yell abusively and to insult the Israelites' God. How should their God be any more able to save them from the all-conquering arm of the Assyrians than had the gods of the nations already cringing beneath the oppressor?

The account of this altercation is in 2 Kings 18¹³–19³⁷ and also in the identical words in Isaiah 36 and 37. What are we to conclude from this fact? Two things. First, here is a typical example of the way in which the Hebrew editor treated his information when he compiled the Books of Kings. He wanted the story of the Rabshakeh and found it already written in the contemporary hand of the prophet. So he took the whole story, word for word as it stood, and sandwiched it into his other sources, just as he did with each piece of information he wished to impart. But the second conclusion is rather more important. We find that the record of the life of the prophet would be incomplete without mention of this incident. He was a preacher, but he was as well an adviser to King Hezekiah —a politician of no mean order. Once again—but this time in a much more systematic way—we find a prophet taking upon himself the direction of the national destiny because he regarded this as a religious duty consistent with his profession as messenger of God to God's people. Indeed, the Book of 2 Kings portrays for us a Hezekiah who was continually striving to act justly and for the best, but behind him stood the prophet whose policy was that Judah was being untrue to God by meddling in world affairs.

Isaiah is one of the great figures of the Old Testament. He was of noble stock and a very acute mind. In the record of his prophecy (most of Chapters 1–39 of our Book of Isaiah. We shall have to see later what was the origin of the rest of the book) there is much which reminds us of the condemnatory tone of Amos, not a little of the wooing tone of Hosea, even something of the fiery challenge of Elijah. But that is combined with the genius of the poet and the vision of the man who has been very near to the reality of God in his thoughts. The account of his visionary call in Chapter 6 is one of the masterpieces of the world's religious literature. It is a picture of a man who felt that he was in the presence of a God who is infinitely *holy*—separate from men; and it is this attribute which he added to the 'justice' of Amos and the 'love' of Hosea. Moreover, Isaiah was an idealist. He was not so happy about the theocratic ideal in his day as the historian was later when he wrote about the same period. But he did believe that the day would come when God would raise up a king who should truly follow in the footsteps of David and lead the people back to their national heritage as the people of God. So, again in exquisite poetry, he longs for the age of righteousness and prosperity which shall come when 'there shall come forth a shoot out of the stock of Jesse [David's tribe] and a branch out of his roots shall bear fruit' (11¹), and bases his optimism on the fact that in Israel they would one day be able to say, 'Unto us a child is born, unto us a son is given; and the government shall be upon his shoulder: and his name shall be called Wonderful, Counsellor, Mighty God, Everlasting Father, Prince of Peace. Of the increase of his government and of peace there shall be no end, upon the throne of David and upon his kingdom, to establish it' (9⁶⁻⁷). It almost looks at first sight as though the prophet were thinking forward to the coming of Jesus; but we are pulled up short when we remember that Isaiah was concerned about the immediate future of Jerusalem, before whose very gates the army of Sennacherib was encamped. (The Christian Church has, of course, been profoundly right in appropriating these majestic words to describe the gift of Jesus to the world.) But it is more probable that the prophet was expressing his conviction that some new-born prince of the house of Judah would turn out to be an ideal king who would lead his nation to a just peace and true prosperity.

Hezekiah was distraught. What should he do? He rent his clothes, but that was no great help in the situation. To Isaiah, the position was clear. Judah had deserved the catastrophe which seemed to be impending, because of her immorality and irreligion, and the Assyrian hordes were the tool by which God should teach her—'the rod of mine anger', as Isaiah calls them (10⁵). All they could

do was to fling themselves upon the mercy of God and
trust Him to work out the problem in His way. Whatever happened, Isaiah believed that a righteous remnant
of the people would be left to establish anew the religious
truths which had suffered by neglect. So strong was this
conviction that he named one of his sons symbolically
Shear-jashub—'a remnant shall return'!

Isaiah never wavered in his belief that God would not
allow His city of Jerusalem to be taken. As the narrative
of Kings suggests, Sennacherib had to withdraw from
the city hurriedly because of a sudden outbreak of
plague—always a bane of Eastern armies before modern
methods of hygiene became known. It was as miraculous
a deliverance for Judah as was the evacuation of Dunkirk
in the last war. There was no further immediate need
for Isaiah to push his policy that Judah should submit
to occupying the position of a small tributary Assyrian
state. The Assyrian records inform us that the vicious
murder of Sennacherib by his sons in his pagan temple
took place twenty years later. The Hebrew chronicler
(2 Kings 19[36-7]) gives us this piece of news at the end
of the story of the siege because it is such an outstanding demonstration in his eyes that all nations are under
the hand of Jehovah! We have to guard against assuming
that such ignoble vindication took place at once. Hezekiah
lived on with Isaiah as his right-hand man, and his
implicit faith in the prophet did not cease when he was
at the very gates of death. Hezekiah's prayer and
Isaiah's prophetic vocation were used by God to bring
healing to the king (2 Kings 20). It is not surprising
to read (2 Kings 18[4]) that the king conducted a 'purge'
of the baal shrines and gave great impetus to true
religion.

All that was counteracted by the work of the next king,
Manasseh, who reigned, as scoundrels so often do in

history, for no less than fifty-five years. The editor is glad to pass over them quickly, for it was an age in which the nation reverted to the old baal worship (partly because men found it difficult to maintain the high moral and religious standards demanded by Isaiah) and Jehovah was looked upon as just one of many gods who were to be worshipped with all the pagan rites of old. Manasseh went further, and took the unprecedented step of shedding the 'innocent blood' of those ardent prophetic people who opposed the new pagan tendencies. The prophet Zephaniah, who lived shortly after his reign, gives us some idea of the state of affairs and preached the vengeance of God upon 'the remnant of baal' and his priests, and upon those who had worshipped the stars.

In 639 there came to the throne the young Josiah, and by a strange chance the influence of the prophetic party was again brought to bear upon the history of the people. Hilkiah, the priest in charge of the Jehovah Temple, and Shaphan, the secretary of state, were superintending certain repairs to the Temple when a roll-book was discovered, which to the experienced eye of the literary man at once appeared as a book of laws. The roll was read to Josiah and he was struck at once by the contrast between the way of life it outlined and that which was the common custom of life at his time. We saw how books of law had always kept an authoritative fascination for the Hebrew since the days of Moses; and the outcome of this discovery was that Josiah set about an eager campaign of destruction of the baal altars and led his people in ordering their lives by the new code of rules. The Temple at Jerusalem became the one central place of worship of Jehovah, and priests were withdrawn from the local shrines and brought to the Temple.

The scholars have adduced a number of reasons for believing that this roll-book was substantially our Book

F

of Deuteronomy (means 'second law' in Greek), and that it was written in secret during the reign of Manasseh by unknown followers of the prophetic party. Perhaps the book as found terminated with the curses outlined in Chapter 28, which may well have caused Josiah to rend his garments. Deuteronomy is not a very interesting book to read; very few legal books are. It really says at great length that man cannot expect to receive the blessing and help of God unless he recognizes that he has certain religious duties towards God and moral duties towards his fellow men. In that, it is very near to the spirit of the Sermon on the Mount, but it lacks the urgency which Jesus put into the moral law. It is in line with all that the prophets have taught us so far of the nature of God, and we shall see that it formed the basis of most of what the future and greater prophets were to say in the next few generations. So we cannot over-emphasize the importance of the discovery of the Book of the Law in 621 B.C. and the consequent reformation of religion which was brought about by the young Josiah. It was ultimately responsible for the continuation of the faith of Israel when it looked as though an age of ignorant paganism had put back the progress of things irretrievably.

But the importance of Deuteronomy is not exhausted by the reformation of 621 B.C. We notice an interesting fact: that the men who re-edited the laws in this book thought it necessary to intersperse them with long historical retrospects, and indeed to place the whole in the mouth of Moses. It looks as though they were deliberately trying to remind us that God and His will were mediated through history. That is exactly the emphasis we should expect. The authors were prophets, and prophecy—as we have seen—consisted in seeing the hand of God in events. There are obvious signs that other pieces of their writings have been woven by the editors into other parts of the first five books of our Bible (the Penta-teuch), and the history of Israel from the Conquest to the Exile (as told in Joshua, Judges, Samuel, and Kings) also bears the stamp of the ideas we find in Deuteronomy. We assume that these books were edited by men who shared the objects of the Reformation of Josiah. To them, for example, we may trace the judgement that kings 'did that which was evil (or right) in the sight of the Lord.' Thus we have an account of the history of this period which goes back to those great religious seers who were peculiar to Israel, the prophets.

Unfortunately, the perennial problem of siding with Egypt or Assyria led to the early death of Josiah. He was killed at the Battle of Megiddo in 608 whilst fighting against the Egyptians, though there seems no clear reason why he should have ventured into such a fray. The narrative of 2 Kings 23[31-34] tells us that Necho, the Egyptian king who killed Josiah, deposed the elected king and replaced him by another son of Josiah, to whom the name of Jehoiakim was given. He was extravagant, and had to exact forced labour to build his ornate palace, which evoked Jeremiah's anger (Jeremiah 22[13-19]) because of its roof-chambers, cedar panelling, and vermilion paint. Events moved swiftly after that. Some few years before, Nineveh, the capital of Assyria, had fallen to the con-quering army of the Babylonians, who were previously part of the Assyrian Empire, but took advantage of the weakness of their overlords to launch an attack against them; and from this time it is the Babylonian kings who ruled the eastern world. The discovery and deciphering of a tablet in the British Museum as recently as 1923 show that the Fall of Nineveh took place in 612 B.C. In 605 the Egyptians were utterly defeated at Carchemish (referred to in Jeremiah 46[2]), and this meant that Palestine passed under the sway of the Chaldean tribes.

Four years later Jehoiakim found that he had to make terms with the conquerors; but in 597 he intrigued, and Nebuchadnezzar of Babylon sent an army to surround the capital, Jerusalem. Jehoiakim died, and left the conduct of the siege to his eighteen-year-old son, Jehoiachin, whose three months' reign ended in the partial reduction of the city by the Babylonians and imprisonment for himself in Babylon, from which he was only released thirty-five years later, after the death of his conqueror. Nebuchadnezzar replaced him by his uncle, whom he called Zedekiah, and to whom he left the government of this subject people.

Once again the situation was met by a prophet, and this time he is the sublimest character in the Old Testament—Jeremiah—much maligned for his pessimism, but quite wrongly. He was a man who faced facts, and in his age there was no place for facile optimism. The situation for Judah was critical in the extreme. How would the spirit of a prophet react to it? Jeremiah was born in the evil reign of Manasseh and belonged to the village of Anathoth in the hills a few miles from Jerusalem. His family were priests, but the shams of priestly ritual he witnessed in his early years gave him a perpetual distrust of the outward forms of religion, and he saw to it that he did not follow the family tradition by becoming a priest. He must have revelled in the stories of the prophets of the eighth century, and much that they proclaimed finds an earnest echo in his own sermons later on.

It was five years before the finding of the Law Book (626) that there appeared to him the vision which persuaded him that he was called of God to be not a priest but a prophet to his people, and which is recorded for us in Chapter 1. He became a preacher of the new ideas of the Law Book, though he later became a violent opponent of those sections of Deuteronomy which stressed

the importance of the correct performance of the ritual
of Jehovah-religion and the predominant place of the
Temple and its sacrifices. But he was not really an important national figure until Jehoiakim came to the throne
(608), when we find him (Chapters 7 and 26) preaching
enthusiastically in the Temple that it was sheer folly for
people to reassure themselves by arguing that the Temple
was God's peculiar sanctuary and so could not possibly
be destroyed by the growing might of Babylon. Only if
they 'oppress not the stranger, the fatherless, and the
widow, and shed not innocent blood in this place, neither
walk after other gods' (7[6]) (how like Amos that sounds!)
shall his people continue to exist as a nation at all. That
declaration resulted in Jeremiah almost losing his life.
Later, for similar oracles, he was put into the stocks, flung
into a pit from which he was only rescued in the nick of
time, imprisoned, half-starved, and often had to remain
hidden for long periods. We can readily understand that
his advice to the nation to submit to the Babylonians
sounded very like treachery, and no man suspected of
treachery is popular with his fellows. But the victory at
Carchemish in 605 proved the truth of Jeremiah's words,
and in the following year he decided to make one frantic
appeal. He secured the services of a friend who was a
capable scribe and not unknown in the precincts of the
palace, Baruch by name, and dictated to him a collection of the oracles which he had previously uttered to
warn the nation of the catastrophe which had now actually taken place. This was taken by Baruch—for it was
not safe for the prophet himself to appear in public—
and read in the outer court of the Temple to all who
would hear. Baruch was questioned by the 'princes' and
taken to appear before the king, who asked him how he
came to write this kind of propaganda. The king was
furiously angry, slit up the leather roll with the knife

which was always attached to it to make any erasures, and flung it into the fire (36$^{14ff.}$). Nothing daunted, Baruch returned to Jeremiah, who dictated the oracles again and added some about the woes which should come to Jehoiakim for his refusal to listen to what had been written for his advice.[1]

We have already seen how, in 597, Nebuchadnezzar first attacked Jerusalem. The next king of Israel, Jehoia-chin, came in for his share of Jeremiah's abuse, and throughout the reign of Zedekiah as puppet king of the Babylonians Jeremiah continued to preach the need for a true conception of God as ruler of all the nations, for uprightness of life, and for a common-sense policy of sub-mission to Babylon instead of the absurd, intense nation-alism of his contemporaries. To symbolize his profound conviction that Israel was under the domination of Baby-lon by the will of God, he went about with a wooden ox-yoke round his neck—a symbol which at least one of the optimists of his time understood. Hananiah, we are told, broke the yoke and declared that the first band of captives taken in 597 would return home within two years (Chapters 27 and 28). From then on, Jeremiah replaced his wooden yoke with an iron one, and also wrote a letter to the captives in Babylon (Chapter 29) advising them to settle in their new surroundings and to make common cause with their captors, preserving the national religion against their future return to their native land. At length the blow fell. Nebuchadnezzar had cause to suspect the loyalty of Zedekiah and came to besiege Jerusalem in earnest. Probably he suspected that there was a movement to ally with Egypt, for the Egyptian king Hophra engaged him in defence of Judah and was defeated. For eighteen months, amid great privations,

[1] The oracles of Jeremiah as they appear in our Bible are not arranged chronologically.

the siege lasted. Then Zedekiah saw that his position was untenable, tried to escape secretly, but was overtaken and treated with the usual Oriental brutality. His sons were slain before his eyes, he was blinded and marched off to join his conqueror's triumphal procession, whilst his city was laid waste (586). Such was the sad end to all the pious hopes of Josiah to recreate the nation as the true people of God.

A governor was appointed to supervise the diminished population in the old city, for all the cream of the nation's manhood was marched off to Babylon. That was the only means ancient monarchs had of enforcing their will upon conquered people, for, unless they depopulated the countries they had taken, revolts could break out and months would pass before the slow communications of those days would bring them any knowledge of the situation. Jeremiah was treated generously by the conquering general, Nebuzaradan, and given the choice of going with the captives or staying in the ruined city with the remnants of the nation. He chose the less attractive alternative and went back, resolved to share the meagre life of the lowest classes, who were left to cultivate the miserable farmsteads on the hills. He threw in his lot with the governor, Gedaliah, and believed that between them they could create out of the scattered remains of the tribesmen a nation which would be morally and spiritually and politically more of an entity than had been the whole nation of Judah. Even in this last hope Jeremiah was doomed to disappointment. Gedaliah was treacherously assassinated by Ishmael, a pretender to the throne of David, whose men, realizing after their deed what would be the consequences when it came to the ears of Nebuchadnezzar, decided to flee the country and set up a new Jewish colony in Egypt. They went to Jeremiah to ask his advice and co-operation. Naturally, he opposed the plan, but when he saw that they were determined to go, he reluctantly went with them and spent the remaining years of his tragic life in a last vain attempt to make them see the reality of religion in human life and the claims of God upon them. He was not very successful in this, and the colony at Tahpanhes has left little evidence of its existence in the annals of history. Tradition says that their prophet perished miserably at the hands of the men he went to help.

So far we have emphasized chiefly Jeremiah's message to his nation in their particular hour of crisis. He is remembered today more for his great human qualities, the fine sense he displayed of loyalty to principle in spite of all the suffering involved, and the new and larger idea of God which was his. No man in the Old Testament drew so near to the bold idea of God which Jesus possessed; and no man's life was more like that of Jesus. We have come to use of Jesus the words Jeremiah first used of himself: 'I was like a gentle lamb that is led to the slaughter' (11[19]). In the intense loneliness to which he was subjected, the prophet thought out the meaning of religion afresh. So far in Israel's history, God's dealings had been thought to be with the nation as a whole, rather than with the individual. Jeremiah made the greatest discovery of all—that God is interested in the life of each individual member of the race, and *his* moral struggles, *his* quest for the highest, *his* personal sense of loyalty are the intimate concern of the God who, as Hosea had taught, infinitely loved all His people. Jeremiah was gripped by the sense of the almost terrifying reality of the power and majesty of God which Isaiah had experienced, and the feeling which all the prophets had in some measure that they were conscripted to serve this divine Ruler, whether they would or no. So he did not say that God was Father. That was left for Jesus to say in every aspect of His life and teaching six centuries later. But, unlike Isaiah and the other prophets, God was for him One who stood in intimate personal relationship, and it is this fact which sets him above all other teachers of Old Testament times.

He had been brought up on the Law of Moses and the sacrifices of the Temple; but these shrank in his mind into lower significance beside the new convictions which came to him of the personal nature of religion. True to the traditions of his upbringing, he enshrined his new teaching in a form of words which would be recognizable to all who heard him speak or read his words in after years. He spoke of a 'new covenant' between God and the individual, which was to generate a knowledge of God more intimate than the national covenant of Moses. Unlike that agreement, it should be engraved on the human heart instead of on tablets of stone; and it would depend upon the moral obedience of the individual to the Law of God. The old ideas had made it so easy to shift the responsibility of one's wrongdoing on the social whole, so that there had grown up a proverb that 'the fathers have eaten sour grapes and the children's teeth are set on edge'—the same primitive thought which found expression in an early record of Moses' Commandments, which spoke of a God who was 'jealous' and would 'visit the sins of the fathers upon the children unto the third and fourth generation of them that hated' Him. How tremendously far all that is from the teaching of Jesus! It was Jeremiah who introduced us to the idea that God makes Himself known as a personal Lord who asks a personal moral obedience. We live in the presence of God and make or mar our lives by the thoughts and actions for which we are ourselves responsible. That means, too, that the individual man is capable of fellowship with God, of understanding something of His will and purpose for the world. It is not possible to estimate how different would have been the history of human progress if Judah had taken to heart the revelation of God which Jeremiah was seeking to interpret to them.

References

Hezekiah and Isaiah: the campaign of Sennacherib— 2 Kings 18^{1}–19^{37}; Isaiah 36^{1}–37^{38}, 8$^{1-4}$, 10$^{5-11}$, 10$^{24-7}$; 2 Kings 20$^{1-21}$.

Isaiah—

The prophet of God's holiness—Isaiah 6$^{1-13}$, 10$^{16-23}$, 25$^{1-8}$, 29$^{15-24}$.

The hope of a King—Isaiah 9$^{1-7}$, 11$^{1-16}$, 26$^{1-8}$, 32$^{1-8}$, 35$^{1-10}$.

Micah 3$^{1-6}$, 4$^{1-5}$, 6$^{1-8}$.

Manasseh's evil reign—2 Kings 21$^{1-18}$; Zephaniah 1$^{1-18}$.

Josiah and the Law Book—2 Kings 22^{1}–23^{27}.

The advance of the Chaldeans—2 Kings 23^{28}–24^{20}.

Jeremiah—

The national adviser—Jeremiah 24$^{1-10}$, 26$^{1-9}$, 32$^{28-44}$.

The life of the disappointed prophet—Jeremiah 1$^{1-19}$, 7$^{1-15}$, 20$^{1-18}$, 28$^{1-17}$, 32$^{6-15}$, 36$^{1-32}$, 37$^{1-21}$.

His letter to the captives—Jeremiah 29$^{1-20}$.

The Fall of Jerusalem and treachery of Ishmael—2 Kings 25$^{1-30}$; Jeremiah 40^{1}–43^{7}.

The new features of religion revealed through Jeremiah— Individual responsibility—Jeremiah 31$^{23-30}$.

The new covenant—Jeremiah 31$^{31-6}$.

Questions for Discussion

1. How did Isaiah differ from Elisha as a political adviser? What development can you distinguish in the form of prophecy between the two men?

2. Whose was the most important contribution to the gradually enlarging idea of God—Amos, Hosea, or Isaiah?

3. See what examples you can find in the Book of Deuteronomy of (i) the importance attached to ritual in religion, (ii) the importance attached to honesty and kindness.

4. Read Deuteronomy 5^{6-21}. This was part of the law upon which Josiah based his reformation. What effects in our modern life are due to the discovery of the book which contains this type of teaching?

5. What do you think of Jeremiah's combined preaching of national policy and religious ideas?

6. Do you think that Jeremiah made the right choice when he decided to remain in Jerusalem in 586? In which country would he have more chance of securing a hearing for his views?

7. How much does our modern faith in God owe to Jeremiah's doctrine of the new covenant?

CHAPTER SEVEN

Babylon—and Back Again

THE RECORD of the history of the dispirited exiles for the next few years is in contrast to the noble idealism of Jeremiah. It was, of course, a tremendous national upheaval; but we should remember that they were only a smallish people, and they were by no means the only people of that age which was uprooted and transferred to other lands. Such things were common in ancient history. What made it so hard for Judah was their intense nationalist feeling. That nationalism was the result of their religion. What bound them together and made them refuse to intermarry with other tribes was their belief that God—their God, Jehovah—was solitary Ruler of their own race, and could not be shared with any other nation.

Now, the men of Judah had lost their national home. The much-vaunted Temple lay in ruins and all its precious vessels and adornments were degraded in the hands of the Babylonians. Nothing could make them feel that life held any meaning now. Jeremiah had prophesied that they would return to their native land after seventy years and had counselled them meanwhile to settle down and prosper in the part of the country which had been allotted to them. They had always been capable businessmen. Now was their opportunity to show what they could do in adversity. But what of that? No; Jeremiah had stayed behind in Jerusalem. It was easy for him, they thought, to tell them what they ought to do in Babylon. They ignored his message of encouragement now as completely as they had previously rejected his prophecy of doom.

In that situation some of the exiles were found on the canal bank by some Babylonians who challenged them in a friendly enough manner to sing some of their national songs. Psalm 137 tells the story of their miserable refusal. How could they sing their national songs, all of which were about Jehovah, when they were in a foreign land? Jerusalem was a charred ruin; there was nothing to sing about now. Then the spirit of vengeance came uppermost, and the psalm goes on to tell how they turned on the Babylonians and reproached them: 'Go on, you can taunt us, but your great city will be destroyed one of these days. Good luck to the race who treats you as you have treated us. Good luck to the man who takes your children and knocks their brains out.' To such depths of vicious bad feeling had the men fallen to whom God's revelation in the prophets had been given. It is no wonder that they did not find it easy to settle down in the new country. They were not slaves, but their own attitude prevented them from making a success of evil days.

Gradually, despair gave way to philosophy. Why had it all happened? Why had God allowed hordes of heathen Chaldeans to ravage the sacred Temple which had been dedicated to Himself? It looked as though evil had won the day and good was defeated, and it is never easy to reconcile that state of affairs with belief in God. That was how the problem appeared to the prophet Habakkuk, who apparently lived in the early part of the Exile. His prophecy is really an early philosophy of history. He states the facts of the Chaldean invasion, and accepts the prophetic position that God must have raised up their armies for His purpose, in spite of the difficulty in believing that. Then he recounts that he had a vision, as a result of which he proclaimed to this people that 'the just shall live by his faithfulness'. He, like Jeremiah and Amos before him, attributed the national calamity to two things, the selfish and unjust practices of the nation as a whole and the worship of graven images.

In all that there is nothing new. But the Exile produced another great prophet who outstripped his fellows in apprehension of God's meaning for men. He is usually known as 'the Second Isaiah' because his prophecies comprise most of the second half of our Book of Isaiah (Chapters 40–55). In ancient days, there were so few books that there was no need to introduce a book with a title or an author's name, for all who could read would have sufficient knowledge to enable them to identify any author's work. A scribe must have copied the oracles of the prophet Isaiah on to a fresh leather roll-book, and then found that when he had finished he had almost as much space left as he had already occupied. So he went on writing other oracles, which everyone would recognize as coming from another preacher; but unfortunately for us the name of this great unknown preacher of the Exile has been forgotten. The most hurried comparison of the tone of the first thirty-nine chapters of Isaiah with the opening words of Chapter 40, 'Comfort ye, comfort ye my people, saith your God. Speak ye comfortably to Jerusalem, and cry unto her that her warfare is accomplished, that the iniquity is pardoned . . .' will show us that we are reading the words of a man whose presuppositions are very different from those of Isaiah. Here is a man with a bright new hope of days to be. Something has happened in world history which has given him cause to look forward to his people's return. Listen as his voice rings out, demanding that the long trek round the Fertile Crescent be prepared for the journey back from captivity to the city of their dreams, Jerusalem: 'Prepare ye in the wilderness the way of the Lord, make straight in the desert a high way for our God. Every valley shall be exalted and every mountain and hill shall be made low: and the crooked shall be made straight, and the rough places plain: and the glory of the Lord shall be revealed, and all flesh shall see it together: for the mouth of the Lord hath spoken it' (40³⁻⁸). For many of us, those words are linked with Handel's *Messiah*, but their first use was among a people who had some hope of release from the restrictions of Babylon and of return to the city of their fathers. We shall see in a few minutes what historical fact gave rise to the Unknown Prophet's shouts of joy; but meanwhile we must notice two important facts about his prophecy.

The first is that there are four sections in which the word 'Servant' is frequently used (42¹⁻⁴, 49¹⁻⁶, 50⁴⁻⁹, 52¹³⁻53¹²). They are generally known as the Songs of the Suffering Servant, and much controversy has waged round their meaning. Nowadays most scholars are agreed that the prophet meant the Servant to represent the nation of Israel, or at least the restored remnant of Judah. It was another answer to the question why God allowed the Exile; and this time the prophet has something new and constructive to say which will do something to reconcile his people to their fate. He sets out that he believes it was God's purpose to let the Israelites go into exile in order to atone in some measure for the sins of mankind as a whole; and that when the nations see the seeming tragedy of the Exile turned into a glorious return, they will be so impressed with what God has done that they will honour both Him and His people Israel. Men can pity Israel, can look upon the nation as 'despised, and rejected of men; a man of sorrows and acquainted with grief'. But the days will come when they will realize the truth: 'Surely he hath borne our griefs, and carried our sorrows: yet we did esteem him stricken, smitten of

God, and afflicted' (Isaiah 53[3-4]). It has always seemed
to me that the prophet had in mind when he wrote this
the life of Jeremiah, who was rejected as a treacherous
dreamer in his own age, but who was later looked upon
as a saint; and that he regarded the life of Jeremiah as
a symbol of the nation of Israel in the world. Later on,
the early Christians came to see that Isaiah 53 had a
peculiarly apt application to the life of Jesus (there is an
example of this in Matthew 8[17]), and Jesus Himself knew
that He was called upon to fulfil the role of the Servant-
Son (Mark 9[12]), but there was no intention in the mind
of Second Isaiah to foretell the sufferings of Christ. Whatever our interpretation of this great passage, it is clear
that it constitutes one of the highlights of God's revelation in the Old Testament. It is exquisite poetry used in
the service of the noblest religious thought.

The second thing to notice is this: We have seen that
the earlier prophets of the seventh and eighth centuries
had moved towards an announcement that the Lord was
the God of all the earth. Amos, for example, had declared that God not only 'brought up Israel out of the
land of Egypt', but also brought 'the Philistines from
Caphtor, and the Syrians from Kir'. Wherever those
places may have been, the prophet is suggesting that the
activity of God is not confined to Israel. But the unknown prophet of the Exile fully grasped the implications
of the fact at which his predecessors were hinting. Here
is the word of God as he realizes it: 'Look unto me, and
be ye saved, all the ends of the earth: for I am God, and
there is none else. By myself have I sworn, the word is
gone forth from my mouth in righteousness, and shall
not return, that unto me every knee shall bow, every
tongue shall swear' (Isaiah 45[22-3]). This is *monotheism*,
absolute and unrestricted—the belief that there is only
one God for all the earth. Here is the noblest peak of all

in the Old Testament announcement of the nature of God. 'Is there a God beside me? Yea, there is no Rock; I know not any', he declares unequivocally (44^8); and then, if that were not sufficient, he goes on to draw a vivid word picture—as vivid a picture as there is in the Old Testament —of a man who cuts down a tree, and with one part of it builds a fire by which to warm himself, with another part roasts an animal for his food, and from the third part carves for himself a god! The same tree is used for fuel and as a means of evoking his worship and fear. It is absurd: no thinking man would consent to such a belief. So at long last, not man's abstruse philosophy, but his sense of humour enabled him to reach the faith upon which our idea of God is built.

There was another great prophet in the days of the Exile, whose work preceded that of the Unknown Prophet, and who had been one of the first batch of captives taken from Jerusalem in 597 B.C. Ezekiel was a fervent admirer of Jeremiah, and constantly repeats his insistence upon the personal relation between God and man. He too quotes the saying about sour grapes (Chapter 18) and enlarges upon his master's conception of the responsibility each man bore for his own misdeeds. He is rather more conscious than Jeremiah of the overwhelming greatness of God, just as Isaiah was, so that there are times when we lose the warmth of Jeremiah's zeal by contrast. But Ezekiel had one supreme conviction—that God would raise up His nation again and make of it the true Israel, greater and more purposeful than Israel had ever been in history; and he felt it was his divinely appointed mission in life to prepare his people for that by keeping ever before them the significant factors of their faith, and especially the details of the ritual of the Temple and its sacrifices, which had been the outward sign of their allegiance to Jehovah through the generations. These details fill

G

many chapters of his prophecy and are apt to be rather dull reading to us. In a weird vision in Chapter 37 he pictures the present distress of his people like a deserted battlefield in a valley, where the enemy has left nothing but the bodies of the slain, which have been stripped clean of all flesh by the vultures. Indeed, the national hopes of Israel had been almost exhausted and they felt themselves as though their nation had ceased to exist. Then in his vision the bones came together at the command of God and gradually took flesh and sinews, until finally they were infused with new life by the breath of God Himself and stood up as a very great army. Thus he believed that God would create a new Israel from the remnants of this captive people. This kind of writing is very strange to us, but in the age of the Exile and afterwards it became very popular in Judaism. In a golden age in the not-far-distant future, Ezekiel taught, God would raise up a leader who would truly shepherd His people among the nations (34¹⁻³¹).

Ezekiel was much more successful in his mission than other prophets had been, largely because his task was one of reconstruction instead of condemnation. He achieved the distinction of being the man who, by his faith in God and his virile belief in the possibility of an early return to Jerusalem, held together the national ideals and set in men's minds the plans for the restored Temple which was to be, and all the minutely ordered details of its worship. Probably his work inspired some other writer or writers to compile the priestly account of the history of Israel which was eventually incorporated in our Old Testament books (see below, p. 106).

We saw that some historical fact during the Exile must have given rise to Second Isaiah's prophecies of hope. We must now turn to see what this was. To the northeast of Babylon, stretching away to the shores of the

Caspian Sea, lay the land of the Medes. In the middle of the sixth century B.C. these doughty warriors swarmed westward across Mesopotamia and captured the city of Haran on the upper Euphrates. They were about to push southwards towards Babylon when they were checked by the sudden attack on their flank by a vassal king of theirs, Cyrus of Persia, whose domain extended east and north-east of the Persian Gulf. This was in 553, and in three years the vassal, Cyrus, was ruler of all the lands of both Medes and Persians. The Hebrew prophets in Exile were not slow to see what effect that would ultimately have upon their own position in Babylon, and it is from this time that we must date the oracles of Second Isaiah. Cyrus is the 'one from the east' in Isaiah 41$^{2-4}$, raised up by God for their deliverance. Cyrus had fulfilled his expectations and attacked and conquered Babylon. Under his enlightened rule the Hebrews were given more consideration, as was only natural, than under their original captors: but the bold, brave hopes of Second Isaiah were never completely fulfilled, nor was the magnificent vision of Ezekiel's restored Temple to materialize for many years to come.

What actually occurred was that in 537 Cyrus issued an edict, of which the substance is preserved for us in Ezra 6$^{1-5}$, giving permission for as many of the captives as wished to return to their native Palestine. But very few took the opportunity to go. After all, fifty years had passed since they were there. Those who had come as young men were too old to go back, and the new generation which had been born in exile did not feel the same concern for Jerusalem as their fathers had felt. So Second Isaiah's dream of the Fertile Crescent thronged with returning Jews singing their songs of praise never quite came true!

Our sources are very confused about the actual sequence

of events, chiefly because they were written two centuries
or more after the events they record and were based on
tradition rather than on written accounts of contemporary
date. But it seems that in 537 B.C. a small number of
stragglers returned to a ruined city and eked out a pre-
carious existence under their leader, Sheshbazzar. There
is more evidence that in 520 B.C. a larger number of people
returned under the leadership of Zerubbabel, who became
the civil governor, and of Joshua, who was destined to be
the high priest; and that they arrived in the still-ruined
Jerusalem to find no signs that the first company had
made a successful colony. The inspiration of this second
return was the enthusiastic preaching of two more prophets, Haggai, who declared that 'the latter glory' of the
Temple at Jerusalem should 'be greater than the former',
and Zechariah,[1] who pictured children playing in the
streets of Jerusalem again and old men leaning on their
staves for very age. The precise dating of these prophecies
enables us to say that the dedication of the restored Temple
took place in 516 B.C.; but after that there was a period
of decline, which is reflected in the message of Malachi,
who endeavoured in an age of disillusionment to recall
his people to a true sense of moral and spiritual values.
The priests, far from being the leaders in the colony,
seem gradually to have grown lax, so that the prophet
announces that Jehovah will indeed come to His Temple,
but with the object of refining it from association with
unworthy elements. The Golden Age, for which they all
yearned, should be a day of judgement. 'Who may abide
the day of his coming? and who shall stand when he
appeareth? for he is like a refiner's fire, and like fuller's
soap' (3²).

[1] Only Chapters 1–8 are thought to be the work of Zechariah himself,
Chapters 9–14 being the work of another prophet whose oracles have
been written on the same roll, as in the case of Isaiah.

The decline was checked by the return in 444 B.C. of Nehemiah, who had held a position of authority in Babylon as cup-bearer to the king, with another batch of Jews who had been invested by King Artaxerxes with permission to rebuild the walls of the ruined city, for which purpose they were to have the assistance of supplies from other subject peoples of the Medo-Persian Empire. Nehemiah seems to have been a very strong character. There was naturally plenty of opposition to his rebuilding on the part of the tribesmen who had occupied the country during the absence of the Jews, and Sanballat and Tobiah the Ammonite are mentioned as typical leaders of ravaging tribes who did their utmost by sporadic skirmishes to hinder the work. But the tenacity and zeal of Nehemiah proved an example to his men, and, by dint of having half of his force ready armed whilst the rest worked, the walls were effectively built. Moreover, Nehemiah seems to have established a virile religious life and an adequate constitution. Later still, in 397, a last leader for returning Jews arose in the person of Ezra, usually given the title of 'the scribe'. He came back to find the walls rebuilt as well as the Temple, and he assumed the task of interpreting the Law of Israel for the new community. Nehemiah 8 informs us that he read the Law solemnly in the ears of all the people. Presumably this was the collection of laws which had been preserved during the Exile by Ezekiel and men of like persuasion; and they became the basis of the new Jewish faith. They are usually known as the Priestly Code, because of their insistence upon the correct ordering of worship as an integral part of religion; and they have been combined with the earlier collections of laws, so that they now form an element in our first five books of the Bible—the Pentateuch. Most of the facts about this period we find in the work of the Chronicler, a later historian who was responsible for editing the books we now know as Chronicles, Ezra, and Nehemiah, though recent discoveries have shown that his sequence of events is not always historically accurate.

The Jews seem to have kept very much to themselves, and insisted upon the strict obedience to the ritual of the Law upon which their faith was based. There were in the north a group of people whose religion was very similar to their own (for they were the descendants of the remnant left behind when the northern kingdom of Israel was taken captive in 722 and of the foreign colonists introduced into the land by the Assyrian kings Sargon, Esar-haddon, and Assurbanipal). But, despite their advances, the Jews would have nothing to do with them because of the impure form of their worship; and these Samaritans, as they were called, ultimately built a rival temple on Mount Gerizim. From that time dates the tradition of mutual hatred which found expression in New Testament times in the phrase, 'the Jews have no dealings with the Samaritans'. Jesus often went out of His way, as in the parable of the Good Samaritan, to shame His contemporaries out of the exclusiveness which was the heritage of Ezra's day.

In spite of this, it was a very happy little community which gathered round the restored Temple. The Book of Psalms, one of the loveliest books of all literature, bears eloquent testimony to the very real sense which the people had at this time of religion as the basis of all life. It is difficult to say when the book as we have it was compiled. It is really a number of collections of hymns, which were brought together by some editor who wished to preserve what was generally remembered from generation to generation. We can best see their meaning if we regard them as the anthems which the various Levitical choirs sang and to which the ordinary worshipper listened in the second

Temple. The headings in the Revised Version give us the names of some of the choirs from whose repertories they were taken—the sons of Korah or Asaph, and so on. Some of the Psalms are called in our Bibles 'Songs of Ascents' ('Songs of Degrees' in A.V.) (e.g. Psalms 120-34). These were sung as the people thronged up the great steps which led to the Temple. We can imagine them listening to the appeal in the words, 'I was glad when they said unto me, Let us go unto the house of the Lord. Our feet are standing within thy gates, O Jerusalem' (Psalm 122[1-2]). In another sense, the Psalms can be regarded as a collection of Jewish prayers, some in public use, others for private meditation. But the point here is that they express, as no other literature does, the true nature of the religion of the men who formed the new Israel after the Exile. The man who could sing that 'Thy statutes have been my songs in the house of my pilgrim- age' (Psalm 119[54]) shows how binding was the Law upon him; whilst from the words of Psalm 6[5] we learn that they had not yet come to believe in a future life beyond death: 'In death there is no remembrance of thee; in Sheol who shall give thee thanks?' At the same time, it is possible that some of the Psalms do date back to the days of David and have been preserved through all the troubled history of the people. We can readily think of David as the author of Psalm 23, 'The Lord is my shepherd'. On the other hand, some psalms illustrate the days of the kings, and still others the later days of the Maccabean Revolt. Some few are psalms which demand retribution for past wrong and express ignoble sentiments which make them quite unsuit- able for use in Christian worship. We find it difficult to share the sentiments of Psalm 68, for example: 'Let God arise, let his enemies be scattered . . . as wax melteth before the fire, so let the wicked perish at the presence of God.'

The despondent captives of 586 were inclined to think

that the Exile meant the end of all their hopes. We have come to see that it developed within them a larger faith and a truer religion, which should in time prepare for the coming of Jesus. They had learned that suffering might be redemptive, as His was to be: they had learned that the God of all the earth had made them the depository of all that was noblest in the world's religion.

References

Conditions of the Exile—Psalm 137.

Habakkuk 1^{1}–2^{4}.

Ezekiel—

The disciple of Jeremiah—Ezekiel 14^{12-23}, 18^{1-32}.

The vision of the new Israel—Ezekiel 37^{1-28}.

The importance of the Temple ritual—Ezekiel 40^{1}–41^{14}.

The Unknown Prophet—

The new hope—Isaiah 40^{1-31}.

Cyrus—Isaiah 44^{21}–45^{8}.

The purpose of Israel's suffering—Isaiah 42^{1-4}, 49^{1-6}, 50^{4-9}, 52^{13}–53^{12}.

God as Ruler of all the earth; the futility of idols—Isaiah 44^{6-20}.

The end of Exile—

Cyrus' edict—2 Chronicles 36^{22-3}; Ezra 1^{1-11}.

Haggai 1^{1}–2^{9}.

Zechariah 1^{1-6}, 8^{1-17}.

Nehemiah 1^{1}–2^{20}, 4^{1-23}.

Ezra 7^{1-28}, 8^{15-36}; Nehemiah 8^{1-12}.

The Psalms, the hymn-book of the Second Temple—Psalms 1, 2, 8, 14, 23, 24, 51, 103, 121–3, 127, 139.

Questions for Discussion

1. What ideas, revealed to the Jews during the Exile, prepared the way for the growth of Christianity?

2. What parts of the teaching of Ezekiel are of importance to Christians?

3. Do you think the Second Isaiah was a greater prophet
than Jeremiah?

4. Compare and contrast Nehemiah with the Pilgrim
Fathers.

5. Do you think Judaism owed more to the preaching of
Haggai and Zechariah or to the legal mind of Ezra?

6. Find half a dozen psalms (other than the Songs of
Ascents) which might have been sung in the Temple
services, and consider how they might have been
used in the worship.

CHAPTER EIGHT

The Jews in the Greek and Roman World

ONE OF the most romantic stories in human history is that of the rise of Alexander the Great. His father, Philip of Macedon, evolved the bold plan of conquering the Persians, who had held sway in the East for 200 years. In 336, when his plan of invasion was almost complete, he was assassinated. But his ideas passed to his twenty-year-old son, Alexander, who crossed the Hellespont, won a great victory against the Persians at Issus (333), wrested the Phoenician seaports from their control and pressed on to Egypt, where he was welcomed and founded the city which afterwards was called Alexandria in honour of him. Then he turned his attentions to the rich lands of the Far East, and eventually died in 323 in his early thirties, having conquered all the territory as far as the border of India. The empire he left was divided between his generals, who proceeded to quarrel among themselves. Finally, two leaders emerged—Seleucus, who ruled the northern part, and Ptolemy Lagi, whose province included Egypt and hence Palestine. Each of these founded a dynasty. Greek influence soon began to be felt among the Jews, who gradually became dispersed over all the Greek-speaking world, until more lived outside Palestine than in it. Greek culture affected them and the Greek language slowly became the normal means of communication. In the third century B.C. it even became necessary for seventy-two elders to translate the Scriptures into Greek. This translation was called the Septuagint (usually represented by the Roman figures LXX for seventy), after the number of men who made it, and it became the chief means whereby the knowledge and appreciation of Judaism spread through the ancient world —for we must notice that the Jew began to influence the Greek world with his ethical and religious ideas almost as much as the Greek influenced him. As Christians, our special interest in the Septuagint version is that it was to be the Bible of the New Testament writers, most of whom took their quotations from it. Hebrew degenerated into a literary language, and it became necessary to write, for use in the synagogues, Targums (or translations of specified portions of the Old Testament) in Aramaic, the common language of the people of Palestine, and the language which Jesus Himself habitually spoke.

In 218 B.C. one of the Seleucid monarchs, Antiochus the Great, started a victorious advance into the Syrian lands, and, though he was defeated by the Ptolemy at the Battle of Raphia in 217, it was not before the government of Palestine had passed into his hands. He was an enlightened ruler, and the Jews welcomed the new régime. His successor, however, precipitated a crisis which was to demonstrate how Jewish religion stood superior to all other. Another Antiochus, whose reign started in 175, adopted a policy of permeating all his domain with the culture of the Greeks—physical, mental, moral, and religious. He was an eccentric though capable ruler who revelled now in magnificence, now in buffoonery, and who called himself Epiphanes, which means 'the god manifest', because he wanted the Greek-speaking world to worship him. His religion, of course, centred in the deities of Olympus, in particular the worship of Zeus; and he did his best to force this cult upon his subject peoples. Now, there was very little difficulty in this for the majority of his subjects, for they believed in a number of gods, and one or more could be added to their pantheon without disturbing their fundamental ideas. But with the Jews it was different.

We have seen how their religion was primarily mono-
theistic and ethical. To them, it was an intolerable blasphemy to suggest that any other god could share with
Jehovah their religious allegiance. At any rate, Antiochus
set up an image of Zeus Olympios in the court of the
Temple. This was in 168. For a time, indignation seethed
and there was no more than passive resistance. We must
recognize that important issues were at stake, for any
compromise on their part would have affected materially
the future of Judaism and in consequence the development of Christianity. There was a need for some courageous leader to vindicate the true faith by which men live.

That leader was found in a most obscure place. Persecution proved ineffectual in stirring the Jews to worship,
so at last Epiphanes sent his officers to order the sacrifice
to Zeus. At a little place called Modin, the official
was met by blank refusal on the part of the priest,
Mattathias, and so proceeded to demand the sacrifice
on the part of the people. One renegade Jew ventured
to obey his behest. Immediately Mattathias killed
both him and the king's officer, and fled to the Judean
hills, followed by his five sons and later by many of
the more earnest Jews, who there raised a guerrilla
band and kept the Greeks at bay. This is known as the
Maccabean Revolt, after Judas the Maccabee (his name
means 'Hammerer'), the son of Mattathias who succeeded
to the command at the death of the priest in 166. This
revolt assumed such proportions that the king had to
send his general Lysias to cope with it; but he was defeated, and three and a half years after the first erection
of the image (165) Judas was able to recommence the
daily offering of sacrifice in the Temple at Jerusalem.

We cannot stay to discuss all the Maccabean rulers.
Three of the five sons of Mattathias ruled in turn, and
they were followed by some other relatives, but none was

so great as Judas. He was a very religious man and a great patriot. The others extended the territory of the Jewish state in a period when the Greeks grew less powerful; and for a time the king was high priest as well. In the succeeding generations the high priest came to occupy the most important place in the community, as leader of the civil and ecclesiastical affairs of the state. This symbolized the belief that politics and religion were for the Jews equally the concern of God.

So far in the Greek period we have not been able to refer to any part of the Bible for knowledge of historical facts. Much of the detail of the revolt is told in the Books of Maccabees in the Apocrypha, that collection of books which were finally refused admission to the Old Testament, because it was felt that they were only of secondary importance as guides for the religious life of man. From 1 Chronicles we can gain some idea of the importance of the Temple in this period; but the book which really shows us the plight and reaction of the nation under the persecution is, strangely enough, the Book of Daniel. This is strange because the book opens with what professes to be a description of the life of several young Jews under the domination of Nebuchadnezzar in the early days of the Exile in Babylon. But there is much else in the account which shows that the book is not intended as a historical record of Babylonian times. For instance, neither Belshazzar nor Darius the Mede occupies anything like the place he actually held in the Empire. There are numerous Persian and several Greek words which would not belong to the early days of the Exile. A large section of the book is written in Aramaic, which, as we have seen, did not become a recognized language until the Greek period; and it is even assumed that the court language in Babylon was Aramaic!

On the other hand, there is distinct evidence that the

book belongs to the period of the Maccabees. The vision of Chapter 8 is a thinly veiled analogy of the historical events of the fourth and third centuries, in which we can clearly distinguish the Persian Empire, represented as a ram, and the Greek Empire, portrayed as a goat. The triumphant progress of Alexander, the disputes of his generals, the rise of Antiochus and the edict of persecution all fit into the allegory perfectly. In Chapter 11 a brief survey of the history is followed by a long description of the reign of Antiochus Epiphanes, culminating in verse 31 with the definite statement that the sanctuary was profaned and the burnt offering replaced by 'the abomination which maketh desolate'—a phrase which is several times used, obviously to suggest the pagan altar of Zeus to which the Jews naturally took such exception. Jesus used the phrase to indicate the reign of paganism in a passage (Mark 13[14]) which we describe as apocalyptic, because it reveals a hidden meaning to those who know what is meant by the phrases used. The phrase 'time, times, and a half' in 12[7] represents the period of three and a half years from 168 to 165 during which the persecution lasted, and the number 1290 in 12[11] corresponds with the actual number of days on which the burnt offering could not be offered because of the Greek domination.

It is not difficult to see, even from these few hints, why scholars have come to assert that the Book of Daniel was in all probability written in 165 B.C., though possibly before the actual death of Antiochus. But why should the book take such an unusual form? That question may be answered generally by saying that it was written, almost in the form of a novel, to inspire and encourage the Jewish people in their resistance of the pagan tendencies of the age of the Maccabees. It is propaganda which would appeal to a people who were enduring alone the perils of religious persecution. The author tells a series of stories about someone called Daniel and his young friends in Babylon, and shows how they were loyal to their convictions in their age, and how neither the lion's den nor the burning fiery furnace had power to hurt them. If they, in face of such opposition, could remain faithful, argues the author, how much more should they of his generation remain true in their persecution to the faith in God which had characterized their fathers? For the time being, God had allowed power to pass into the hands of a hostile emperor. The reason for God's action remained a mystery. But one thing was sure. In due course, when God chose, the sufferings of His people should prepare for His real victory, for 'the Most High ruleth in the kingdom of men'. This style of writing, so unreal to us, was extremely popular in the centuries before the coming of Christ, and was called 'apocalyptic', or 'revealing'. We can readily understand that it would not be safe to speak in undisguised terms of the iniquities of Antiochus, for which ancient cruelty would have quickly found an adequate punishment. But the people did find encouragement in the vivid imagery of books like Daniel.

The 'holy commonwealth' of the Jews prospered under the later Maccabees, though it was politically a period of intrigue and unrest. Jerusalem became the centre of the spiritual aspirations of the race rather than the political capital. The success of the Maccabean Revolt made men realize that in their religion they had a foundation such as no other people possessed. Religion, indeed, became the dominant idea of the time. Men took their beliefs seriously. Chief among them were the Pharisees, the people who, as their name implies, separated themselves from the majority of their fellows by stricter obedience to the details of religious observance. They were not at this period a particular class indulging in a super-excellent degree of holiness; for the tradition of Israel was that the whole nation was holy, devoted to God. But at the beginning of the first century B.C. they constituted that part of the nation which regarded the Torah, the Law, as the very basis of all the life of the nation and of the individual. There was not one set of moral commandments for national life and another of individual requirements; the two were one. The time came when the Pharisees destroyed all the joy in religion and brought upon themselves the hearty condemnation of Jesus for their absurdly strict insistence upon the letter of the Law rather than its spirit. But Jesus does not accuse them of irreligion. The Law was for them so binding in importance that they came to wear phylacteries—little leather cases strapped round the forehead and the fingers of the left hand which contained the 'Shema'—the daily Jewish prayer from Deuteronomy 6[4-9]—and tassels on the border of their shawl-like garments, each tassel being supposed to remind them of some one of the many commandments of the Law. Jesus refers to them in Matthew 23[5], suggesting that the merely outward demonstration of loyalty to the Law was by no means sufficient. But that charge could not justly be laid against the earliest Pharisees, or Hasidim, as they were called.

They were the recognized leaders of the people, mostly coming from the poorer classes of society, but forming a true aristocracy of learning. They were not priests, but laymen who were really concerned about the fundamentals of religion. They worked in collaboration with the Scribes—the professional rabbis who spent their time in long discussions as to the meaning of the ancient Law for their own times. The difficulty was that most of the Law had been written for a nomad people, whose problems were entirely different from those of the civilized community which found itself in Palestine in this age. What did the Law imply for this age? The Law, for example, rejected work on the Sabbath; but the Scribes had to define exactly what constituted work. The disciples of Jesus were accused of 'breaking the Sabbath' because they rubbed ears of corn in their hands on the way from the synagogue; and Jesus was watched to see whether He would heal on the Sabbath. Healing on the Sabbath was lawful only if life was in actual danger, they said. Just as the Pharisees became over-zealous for the religion of the book, so the Scribes became over-fastidious in their interpretations. But in the age with which we are dealing at the moment both Scribes and Pharisees were popular. They were admired as the intelligent section of the community, and every Jewish mother would be proud if her son joined the Pharisee party, and undertook the necessary study it entailed. It was in one sense roughly comparable to the status accorded in this country to a man who has been to a university.

Opposed to the Pharisees were the Sadducees, though they had much less influence on the politics of the day. Several rulers found how impossible it was to secure the support of the country unless they sided with the Pharisees. The Sadducees were few in number and rejected the strict developments of the Law on the part of the Pharisees. Generally speaking, they came from the priestly or noble sections of society, were more liberal in their outlook in politics, but more conservative in their religious notions, rejecting such new beliefs as that in the resurrection. A third party were the Essenes, fanatical rigorists who laid much store by ritual washings, ceremonial purity, and observance of the festivals, and who at the same time practised severe moral restraint, emphasizing the importance of truthfulness, charity, and self-control.

This age, too, saw the large development of the synagogue as a place of worship and teaching. Previously we have observed that the ritual of the Jewish religion centred

H

in the great Temple in Jerusalem. To this all Jews continued to make their pilgrimage, when they could, for the great festivals of thanksgiving and the Day of Atonement; but ever since the Exile, scattered colonies of Jews throughout the world, as well as in Palestine, had felt the need for some place where they could worship the God of their fathers. So the Temple gradually became merely the place of sacrifice, whereas every little town had its local synagogue, where the Scriptures (that is to say, the collection of Law books and Prophets) were read in public, prayer and praise were offered to God, and where during the week the rabbi or teacher was responsible for what education the children got, chiefly learning to read Hebrew. Jesus Himself must have received no more than a synagogue education, and we can see from many stories in the Gospels what an important place the synagogue occupied in the life of every ordinary man and woman.

The centuries before the coming of Jesus are noteworthy as a period of great literary activity. There had been various documents written at different periods and containing the history and laws of the people, each stressing some different aspect. The earliest of these was the prophetical history, and probably dates from as far back as 850 B.C., the era of Elijah, and is often designated by the letter J, because its name for God was Jehovah, and it derived from Judea. A parallel account, usually called E, was compiled also by the prophetic bands in the northern kingdom (often called Ephraim) about 750 B.C. It described God by the Hebrew word *Elohim*. Then there was the Deuteronomic history, discovered, as we have seen, in 621 B.C., and known as D; and the priestly history, dating from the Exile and known as P. These had been re-edited until they formed the historical and legal books which make up the first part of our Bible.

To these had by now been added the collection of the Prophets (which included the Books of Samuel and Kings), though nobody seems to have said officially which books should be included in the collection and which omitted. They just came to be accepted by common consent. So the Old Testament comprised by this time two main sections—the Law and the Prophets—and thus it continued until the time of Jesus. He declared in the Sermon on the Mount that He came not to destroy the Law and the Prophets, but to fulfil them.

The third section—the Writings—consisted of the poetical books, such as the Psalms, then coming into general use, Job, a poetical answer to the problem of the suffering of the innocent given by a writer of the fifth century B.C., but very inadequate to our way of thinking, and Proverbs, the collection of wise sayings of the sages. At the end of this section—though in our English Bible it comes after the Book of Kings—was placed the Book of Chronicles, a later and idealized historical account. (These historical books—Samuel, Kings, Chronicles—constituted single books in the Hebrew version, but were divided into 1 and 2 Samuel, etc., by the translators of the Septuagint.) It was not until the end of the first century A.D. that the Council of Jamnia finally declared that these books too were worthy of inclusion in the canon of 'Scripture', but during the Greek period they must have gained popularity and general recognition.

There is one other little book, probably written in the third century B.C., which gives us an insight into the broadening ideas of the Jewish people. It is the Book of Jonah. Most of us know little or nothing about it except that it is an unbelievable story about a fish swallowing a man and afterwards depositing him alive on the shore. If that were all the book contained, it would never have been counted worthy of a place in the Bible, which reveals the very nature of God. But the book is much bigger than that. The fish is mentioned in only one or two verses, and the author never intended for one moment that thinking men should take literally something which to him was an allegory, like *The Pilgrim's Progress*. We don't take out an atlas to look for the site of Bunyan's Doubting Castle. It is just as absurd for men to worry their heads over the impossibility of the story of the fish, or the miraculous growth of Jonah's gourd.

Briefly, the story is that a man called Jonah was called of God to undertake missionary work in Nineveh, the pagan capital of the violent Assyrians. He felt himself incapable of doing the job; and, since he was a henotheist (i.e. he thought Jehovah's rule only extended over Israel and Palestine, not over the rest of the world), he tried to avoid his responsibilities by taking ship for a foreign port. On the voyage, a storm arose, which was attributed by the superstitious sailors to the presence on board of some fugitive from justice. Jonah's conscience troubled him, and, when they discovered the reason for his voyage, he was thrown overboard. The fish swallowed him, but after three days replaced Jonah on dry land. There he again experienced the divine call to go to the Ninevites, and this time he obeyed, with the result that the whole city repented and was not punished by God. When Jonah came to think this over, he felt it very unjust and he was angry with God. He sat down and a shrub grew up to shelter him, and then as quickly shrivelled up in the wind. Jonah was angry again; but God appeared and suggested to him that if Jonah was concerned about a shrub which he had no hand in making, it was right and proper that God should have infinite pity and concern for the people of Nineveh who were His own creation.

We have been able to see from our study of the slowly developing history of the Hebrews that it was evidently the supreme purpose of God in choosing the Israelite people to use them as His instrument for spreading the knowledge of Himself among all men. In every successive age they were far and away in advance of the religious ideas of their neighbours. They had the noble teaching of the prophets when other tribes were still practising human sacrifice, and hundreds of years before our own forefathers gave up using woad. But, far from sharing their faith with the whole world, their history shows them to have grown gradually more exclusive. It took the Exile (just as it took Jonah the period inside the fish) to make them realize their true responsibility as guardians of the truth of real religion and missionaries whose task was to bring all men to a knowledge of God's real concern for them. With that in mind, and remembering that the book is an allegory, Jonah assumes an entirely new meaning. It is to be interpreted as an appeal to the Jews of the Greek period to break down their narrow exclusiveness and to proclaim the truth about God to all the world. Nineveh represents the whole pagan world. God has no desire to wreak vengeance upon the world for its evil ways, but He does desire that men everywhere should see His long struggle through history to bring them into friendly relationship with Himself. Israel had been taught the truth herself, and none was more fitted to teach others. They could not ultimately escape their responsibility, any more than Jonah's voyage proved to be an escape. The guiding hand of God is seen in the Exile, as in His provision of the fish in the allegory.

So Jonah is the only missionary book in the Old Testament, and the tragedy is that its message, like that of so many of the prophets, went almost unheeded. Here and there in the century before Christ we find Jews who were letting other men see that their religion was part of the world's heritage of truth and not some peculiar preserve of a very particular people. An occasional zealous enthusiast would 'compass sea and land to make one pro-selyte'—a convert from heathenism to the Jewish faith. But there was no general movement of opening the way for all men to enter the closed community of the Jewish church. The picture Jesus drew in His parable of the Pharisee who thanked God that he was not as other men are was not a fantastic overstatement of the case.

In spite of that, however, men in the Greek world did come to see that the high ethical teaching of the Jews was an infinitely better way of life than their own, and that the belief in one supreme God over all was more satisfying to the human intellect than their haphazard belief in the hero-gods who gorged themselves on nectar on the heights of Olympus and were less moral than those who worshipped them. Many of the greater thinkers among the Greeks allied themselves with the Jewish syna-gogues to learn about the Law and to attend such services as they were allowed, though of course they could not become Jews by race. These people were called 'God-fearers'. Lydia of Philippi (Acts 16[14]) was one of them, and they are often mentioned as among Paul's earliest converts to Christianity.

We must now leave the Greeks and take up the history of the people again where we left it at the decline of the Maccabees. In 69 B.C., on the death of the queen, two of the descendants of the Maccabees quarrelled over the succession—Aristobulus, supported by the Sadducees, and Hyrcanus, championed by the Pharisees. War resulted. Just at that time Pompey, the Roman general, was re-turning from his victorious campaigns in the east against Mithradates, and both parties appealed to him to arbi-trate. He marched down, decided in favour of Hyrcanus, and then found the situation complicated by a third party of fanatics who wanted to do away with the monarchy and be ruled by the priests only. With typical Roman thoroughness, Pompey marched to Jerusalem, stormed the Temple, and Jewish independence was at an end. Palestine became tributary to Rome, with Hyrcanus left as high priest, but not as king, and responsible to the Roman governor of Syria. (63 B.C.) On the whole, the Romans governed well, though they never found the province an easy one to manage. In time an Edomite king called Antipater gained power in the land, and after his death his capable son, Herod, who had been educated in Rome, was made king by the Romans (37 B.C.). He was an excellent ruler in many ways, and did his best to ingratiate himself with the Jews by undertaking in 20 B.C. to rebuild the Temple. That task was not finished until A.D. 64, and we have a picture in the gospels of Jesus and His disciples admiring the progress of the work since their last visit to the capital (Mark 13[1]). Herod kept excellent order in the country, but for many reasons the Jews hated him. He was callously cruel, often crucifying and burning offenders, his taxation was oppressive, and he was desperately suspicious. He was just the type of man who would have been expected to slaughter the innocent children at Bethlehem when he suspected that his throne was in danger from the birth of another king (Matthew 2[16]). The main cause of their hatred, though, was that he was a foreigner—a cursed Edomite, whose interest in their religion was only superficial, who built Greek temples in other cities as he had built the Jewish Temple in Jerusalem, and who introduced the pagan customs of Greece whenever he could.

After his death in 4 B.C. the country was divided into four tetrarchies, three of them ruled by his relatives, and from A.D. 6–41 the real ruler in Palestine was the procurator, a Roman official who was responsible for order and civil law, whilst the religious government of the country still resided in the high priest, who held office under the Romans. Pontius Pilate, who was procurator from A.D. 26–36, was typical of these governors of the country. He was merciless, vacillating, vicious; he would subdue revolt by mass executions, and would pursue any policy which would keep the country at peace for a short while. He, like all Roman officials, despised the Jews, and found them cantankerous and ready to riot for the least cause. They, on their side, were proud and openly contemptuous of the Romans, whom they regarded as 'sinners of the Gentiles' and infinitely inferior to themselves. Were not they the people of God? For a while, the Sadducees and the small number of the Herodians—supporters of the Herod régime who believed in the Roman government—tried to keep the peace, but they were hopelessly outnumbered. The Pharisees were again the dominant political party, and they were respected by the common people, whilst the more adventurous spirits joined the Zealots, a revolutionary party which was pledged to smash the Roman yoke by every means, constitutional or otherwise, and to whom shedding Roman blood became a sacred duty.

It was easy to see what must have been the outcome of such folly. The might of Rome would never submit to such insubordination. The only wonder is that the climax was so long delayed. But in the end Vespasian advanced into the country in order to crush rebellion (A.D. 67). By stages, he subdued the country in the north, and left his son Titus to besiege Jerusalem. The Zealots and some of the Pharisees went to extremes of fanaticism, and the final battle was fought out in the Temple itself. The Pharisees and Zealots, having endured starvation and pestilence, barricaded themselves in the Temple and then Titus' men set fire to it (A.D. 70).

Very briefly, that is the background of the life of Jesus.

It was an age of distrust, hatred, intrigue, revolt and cruelty. So far as religion was concerned, it was an age of misunderstanding, unreality, and misguided faith in a God who was expected to raise up a leader to bring unity and victory to a disordered people. All the continued revelation of the nature and purpose of God through the history of the centuries had failed to awaken in the people of Israel any higher response than their profound yet misguided nationalism. The final revelation was still to come in the person of Jesus Christ.

References

(The passages which belong to this chapter are mainly illustrative of the period, rather than historical accounts of it. The main work which gives the Jewish point of view of the history is the Jewish historian Josephus' *Wars of the Jews*, Books 1 and 2, which can be found in most public libraries. The account of the Wars of the Maccabees is in the Book of 1 Maccabees in the Apocrypha, which was written in Hebrew by an orthodox Jew shortly before the birth of Jesus.)

Daniel 1^{1-21}, 3^{1-30}, 5^{1-31}, 6^{1-28}, 7^1-8^{14}, 12^{1-13}.

Jonah 1^{1-17}, 3^1-4^{10}.

Questions for Discussion

1. Do you agree that it was in the age of the Maccabees that the Jews really became aware of the uniqueness of their religion?
2. What do you gather from the Book of Daniel about the 'underground movement' of opposition to Antiochus?
3. Compare and contrast the Book of Jonah and *The Pilgrim's Progress* as religious allegories.

4. Is it true to say that missionary activity is the surest sign of a live religion? Were the sixth century A.D. (when Roman missions first came to England) and the early nineteenth century (when most of our modern missionary societies were founded) the periods of strongest Christian faith? In the light of your discussion, try to decide why Judaism was both successful and unsuccessful in the two centuries before Christ.

5. Trace the direct and more remote causes of the decline of the people which culminated in the Fall of Jerusalem in A.D. 70. What was wrong with the national ideas?

6. How and why would early Christianity make more impression on the world and prove more satisfying than Judaism in the first two centuries A.D.?

CHAPTER NINE

The Fulfilment of History

THE HISTORY of Israel for at least 1,500 years has shown us the inescapable fact that God was trying to make a particular people know what He is really like. It was not for nothing that they came to be called 'the chosen race'. The judgement of events yields that conclusion and none other. God intended them to be the medium for spreading knowledge about Himself to men beyond the borders of Israel. The prophets belonged to Israel alone, and to them must be accorded a position of pre-eminence in revealing God to men. But the Law revealed God, too, for it enshrined for all time the moral code by which God who was just and real should be served. And history revealed God, for no thoughtful man could read the history of the people without bias and fail to see the concern of God for the men He had called into being. Not only that, but there were spiritual seers who knew by that undeniable intuition of the inner life that God had intimate relations with them. 'He made known his ways unto Moses, his doings unto the children of Israel' (Psalm 103⁷).

But if the curtain had to be rung down on the miserable tragedy of A.D. 70 (when Titus of Rome conquered Palestine and put an end to their national ambition), it would have seemed that the history was incomplete. In fact, it would rather have given the lie to the spirit of development we have been trying to trace all through. It would have meant that God had failed—or, alternatively, that the history was just a fortuitous collection of events, and that we had quite wrongly interpreted them to mean that God was speaking consistently to men. It is possible to reach that conclusion only if we ignore the fact of Jesus—a fact which is established upon the most trustworthy historical data, abundantly documented, which criticism has never been able to destroy. Not only have we the testimony of four of His followers in the Gospels, but Josephus, the Jewish historian, and the classical writers, Pliny, Tacitus, and Suetonius, add their witness to the fact that Jesus lived in Palestine in the first century of this era. Incidentally, we have more ancient manuscripts of those Gospels than of any of the Latin or Greek classics whose integrity is never seriously questioned.

Jesus was both the fulfilment of history and God's final Word to men. That is to say, in Him we find the teaching of all the years brought to a focus and applied to human life; and at the same time we see that God was saying something to men in Him which was greater than anything men had realized so far—something which, though history should progress and man's understanding of the universe had only started, should be for ever valid as an expression of the truth about God. There were many revelations of God in the past and there will be more in the future, but what was revealed in Jesus was unique. That impression is amply confirmed by the appeal which the life of Jesus has always made to men, whether they are the simple disciples who flocked around Him in the first place or the people of every class and nation and age who find in Him now the meaning of life and the inspiration of all adventurous thinking and action. We must leave Jesus to make His own appeal to us. It is not the purpose of this chapter to attempt to outline the life of Jesus. But, just as we tried to get a general picture of the development of religion in the Old Testament so that we could fit into the complete scheme the stories we have heard separately through the years, so we ought to know something of the principles of the teaching and the life of Jesus, so that we can fit into that scheme the stories we know about Him—and, naturally, because we are Christians our knowledge of the stories of the Gospels will be more thorough than our knowledge of the Old Testament stories.

Jesus was born during the reign of Herod the Great (according to Matthew's Gospel), who died in 4 B.C. The date usually assigned to the birth of Jesus is 6 B.C. (There was some bungling of the dates when the Roman monk Dionysius Exiguus came in the sixth century to fix the date we now use. He chose the wrong year for the birth of Jesus and consequently for the opening of the Christian era.) Politically, it was an uncomfortable time. When Jesus was in His teens, Judas the Gaulonite raised revolt against a new edict of taxation, which he said 'was no better than an introduction to slavery', and he was never really defeated, but there were sporadic outbreaks of banditry and desperate fighting until the final great revolt of A.D. 66, which led to the coming of Vespasian to sack the country. Jesus spent His youth in an environment of revolution. Jewish peasant and Roman official lived side by side in mutual distrust and hatred. The proud nationalism of the ages had left a heritage of indomitable ferocity which was likely to blaze up at any provocation. On the other hand, the Romans were ever tactless and unsympathetic with Jewish ideals.

To Jesus, it all appeared as folly that the nation should jeopardize its very existence when an attitude of tolerance on both sides would have made for peace. But the Pharisees, the popular party still, and the emotional Zealots had sworn eternal enmity to Rome, and nothing the more moderate Sadducees and Herodians could do would stem the tide of revolt. When Jesus commenced His ministry, these two parties sought continually to involve Him in their respective arguments. One of the most famous examples of this is when the Pharisees made a temporary pact with the Herodians, the party which favoured submission to Rome, and sent them to Jesus to ask whether it was 'lawful' for Jews to pay the Roman taxes (Matthew 22[15-22]). If He said 'No', the Herodians would accuse Him of disloyalty to Rome, whereas if He said 'Yes' the Pharisees would accuse Him of supporting the claims of Rome, which they regarded as a pagan tyranny seeking to overthrow the rule of God. The answer Jesus gave made clear His belief that both God and the State have legitimate demands to make upon their subjects, and that He was primarily concerned that man should not forget his rightful duty to God; for it was an easy matter to make religious scruples an excuse for non-observance of duty to the State. In the very next paragraph (Matthew 22[23-33]) we find that the Sadducees, enheartened by the failure of the Pharisees to secure Jesus' support for their nationalist views, came to Him with a question about resurrection. This is a very good illustration of the way in which questions of politics and dogma were discussed from the same point of view of religion. We are not at all used to hearing the ethics of inland revenue discussed from the pulpit: the Jew was. The Roman officer could conscript a Jew to carry his bag along the road—an enactment which only made the Roman yoke more degrading to bear. Jesus wanted men to regard even this as a means of showing their friendship, so that they would be prepared to go two miles with the man who could command them to go one (Matthew 5[41]), but it was not likely that such teaching would be received favourably in such an age.

The Roman genius for government more often than not overlooked the differences of national temperament and individual personality. From their point of view, all was well if a country was subdued and if the taxes were regularly forthcoming. The system of tax-farming was undoubtedly corrupt, but Rome was only concerned that it was capable of producing the required revenue. A man was appointed to collect each of the several taxes in each town of any size, and, though it was not necessarily true of the tax-collector in the days of Jesus that he paid down a lump sum and then proceeded to extort however much he could over and above this sum, it was naturally looked upon as a degrading occupation. If a man got rich, it must have been because he cheated his fellow Jews. For a Jew to engage in such a system meant that he did not share the popular antipathy to Rome: it meant that he did not believe, as most of his nation did, that God was soon to destroy the Roman power in Judea. Hence such a man had no part nor lot in the synagogue, and strict Jews would not eat at his table. Publicans are always linked in the Gospels with the moral 'sinners' and shared the opprobrium of the despised class. Jesus had no place for such an attitude, but made one tax-collector, Matthew, a member of the apostolic band, and went out of His way to dine both with him and with Zacchaeus, the chief publican of Jericho. For this gracious friendliness, He was dubbed 'a gluttonous man and a wine-bibber, a friend of publicans and sinners'.

On the positive side, the Jew of the age of Jesus inherited a profound belief in the prophetic message that God should raise up a king who should lead them back to prosperity and independence. This idea, which had started with the prophecy of Isaiah, had grown in breadth and in importance since the Exile, and now the rabbis read a new and more urgent meaning into it in view of the Roman occupation of the land. Once again they were an oppressed people, though they failed to recognize the undoubted benefits of good government—military security, excellent roads, and public works—which they gained

from the Roman occupation. So side by side with the
fanatical nationalism of the Zealots there grew up a strong
belief in the early coming of a leader, who should gather
round him all the forces of opposition and should once
again establish the Jews as a free people. He was not
always thought of as a supernatural leader (that is why I
have not used capital letters in speaking of him in the last
few sentences), but there were to be supernatural events
to herald the programme of deliverance. The leader
was to be divinely-appointed—the Messiah (which is really
the past participle of a Hebrew verb and means 'the
anointed one', just as the Greek word from which we
derive our name 'Christ' means the same). So the people
of Israel should really become a theocracy (or 'folk
governed by God'); for God, through the appointed
leader, would truly become Ruler of His people, though
in a larger sense than any of the Old Testament writers
had imagined. The prophets had spoken of a descendant
of the house of David who should rule Israel; so every
Hebrew mother who could claim any kind of descent
from David longed that she should be chosen of God to
be the mother of the Messiah. (Hence Matthew's great
care in his first chapter to prove by a long genealogy
that Jesus could trace His family tree back to David.)

Talk of a Kingdom was common. Jesus was not the
first to use the phrase 'Kingdom of God'. It was on the
lips of the most influential of the rabbis. We have both
in the New Testament and in the contemporary narrative
of Josephus the record of the enthusiasm which swept
through Judea as a result of the preaching of John the
Baptist. He was not a Christian, but a Jewish reformer
who could not entirely agree with the rabid excesses of
the Zealots, but who took his stand by the faith that God
would raise up a King, for whose coming the people
needed to undergo a thorough moral reformation. So we

see him standing with his camel-hair cloak, begging men
to mend their ways, for they would not be ready to fulfil
the purposes of God unless their individual morality came
up to the high standard demanded by the prophets, the last
of whom John undoubtedly was. In a very real sense, then,
John the Baptist prepared the way for the coming of Jesus.

Jesus was nearly related to John, and for some considerable time joined his band of followers, actually sub-
mitting to the rite of baptism to express His allegiance
to the principles for which John stood and to show, by
partaking of a custom by which pagan converts (or pro-
selytes) were apparently admitted to the Jewish faith,
that He was closely bound up with the hopes and aspirations of His own nation and the ordinary men of His day.
The Fourth Gospel account (John 1$^{29-36}$) makes it clear
that John regarded Jesus as more than one of his ordinary
disciples; and that goes some way to explain why, when
John was put into prison, Jesus Himself set out as a teacher.
Indeed, He took over some of John's associates, men who
must have known Him intimately in John's company—
a fact to remember when we try to understand why Simon
and Andrew and James and John so readily left their
fishing to go with One who simply walked up to them
on the lakeside and said, 'Follow Me.'

Moreover, Jesus took over the word 'repent', which had
been the keynote of John's proclamation, but He added
to it the phrase which was to express the significance of
His own message—'for the kingdom of heaven is at hand'
(Matthew 4^{17}). (Matthew, like the true Jew that he was,
always tried to avoid mention of the sacred name of God
if he could. So, instead of speaking of 'the kingdom of
God'—as do the other Evangelists, Mark and Luke—he
conveys the same idea by representing it as the Kingdom
belonging to Him whose throne is in the heavens, i.e. 'the
kingdom of heaven'.)

I

What did Jesus mean by the Kingdom? Was it to be a sort of golden age to come gradually in the future, when all good men's dreams should come true and in some glorious way suffering and injustice should give place to universal happiness and equity? Or was it some catastrophic intervention by God into the established order of things, which should bring about a perfect state of world government according to the omnipotent will of God? The foremost New Testament scholars today insist that Jesus meant neither of these two opposites—neither the evolutionism of the former nor the revolutionism of the latter. Dr T. W. Manson writes (*Teaching of Jesus*, p. 117): 'Whether we think of the New Jerusalem as something to be built in England's green and pleasant land or as descending complete and perfect from Heaven, we totally misconceive its nature if we imagine it as a glorified garden suburb, or, in a more refined way, as somewhat akin to the ideal polity of the philosophers.'

Generally speaking, Jesus used the phrase 'Kingdom of God' to imply neither a particular place or time, nor yet a state of affairs. He certainly did not mean it to describe the heaven of the after-life. He was thinking neither in geographical nor in political imagery. The rabbis spoke of 'taking upon oneself the *malkuth* of heaven', by which they meant the scrupulous observance of the Law, or Torah. Jesus said: 'Whosoever does not receive the *malkuth* of God as a little child shall not enter into it' (Mark 10[15]). Surely He meant that God's sovereign rule was a relationship more real and personal than that exercised by the Law. It is interesting that the references to the Kingdom become more frequent in the Gospels after Peter's spontaneous confession at Caesarea Philippi that Jesus was 'the Christ, the Son of the living God'. That revelation of what has been called 'the Messianic secret' is the great watershed of our Lord's ministry. It created a new relationship between Him and His disciples. They were accustomed to respect Him as Teacher: now they were compelled to revere Him as King—and such a King as evoked the supreme loyalty due only to God. When the disciples first answered the question, 'Who say ye that I am?' the Kingdom had in one sense come, for Jesus brought the Kingdom in coming Himself to men. This is what Jesus meant by saying, 'The kingdom is within (or among) you.' The Kingdom is that personal relationship between God and man which acknowledges the authority of God to claim from man complete loyalty and obedience. Whenever an individual accepts this sovereignty, he 'receives the Kingdom of God' in the sense of the Gospels. That is why the parable picture of the wedding feast (Matthew 22¹⁻¹⁴) can be likened to the Kingdom of Heaven. The guest who refused to wear the host's proffered wedding garment (a special *khalil* was always provided in the East for each guest, and each was expected to wear it as a sign of respect and loyalty) was typical of those who wanted to accept the benefits Jesus brought to men without in return giving the obedience which admits that He has the right and the power to rule their lives in every respect. In several places in the teaching of our Lord we are warned about the penalty of disloyalty to that declaration of the will and nature of God which was made in Jesus Christ. The parables of the sheep and goats (Matthew 25³¹⁻⁴⁶) and of the money given in trust (Matthew 25¹⁴⁻³⁰) both make it clear that the King is also our Judge. In a very real sense, we, who have received the priceless heritage of the Biblical revelation of God, must render account of our stewardship. In the Bible, and most of all in Christ, we are confronted with the Word of God for us—His purpose and will. How have we responded to that tremendous declaration? The words of John's Gospel are fearful in their directness: 'This is the judgement: that the light is come into the world, and men loved the darkness rather than the light; for their works were evil' (John 3^{19}).

But there are occasions in the teaching of Jesus when the Kingdom is said not to be a present reality but to lie in the future. 'The Kingdom is not yet.' It is like a projected marriage for which the bridesmaids have to wait with lamps trimmed (Matthew 25$^{1-13}$). In the parable of the sheep and goats it is associated with judgement and a coming of the Son of Man in His glory with the angels. 'Many shall come from the east and the west, and shall sit down with Abraham, and Isaac, and Jacob, in the Kingdom of heaven' (Matthew 8^{11}). Jesus, like the best of the rabbis, looked forward to the 'Day of the Lord' when God's sovereign rule over men should be consummated. This is what is meant by 'the coming of the Son of Man'. Paul, in a telling word-picture of this consummation, pictures Christ having subdued every power hostile to His reign and handing over the Kingdom to God the Father in order that God may be 'all in all' (1 Corinthians 15$^{20-8}$).

This is a realm in which metaphor—picture-language— is the only possible means of expressing ideas. If, in His teaching, we find that Jesus referred to the Kingdom as both present and future, that is because its final consummation is the inevitable corollary of its coming in His person as an expression of the eternal sovereignty of God. The Kingdom became the dominant conception of His teaching, but it was a very different Kingdom from that for which the peasants of Galilee generally hoped: for when He saw (John 6^{15}) that there was danger that the people would take Him and make Him King according to their own ideas, He fled lest the whole purpose of His mission should be betrayed by misunderstanding enthusiasts. The Kingdom can grow within a man like a grain of mustard seed. It can equally be discovered suddenly like hidden treasure or a precious pearl. This is the ever-recurring wonder of religion. God claims one man's loyalty in one way, another's quite differently. In His sight we are not like so many peas in a pod, but are individuals whose wills are their own to make them His. It is in that thought that the idea of the Kingdom leads on to the other great stress of our Lord's teaching—that God is Father.

Jesus' main concern is that we should recognize the fact that God is King, and it is His character which makes the Kingdom what it is. He is in virtue of that position capable of commanding men's allegiance, but instead it is of the very essence of the divine rule of human life that His subjects should enter voluntarily into a state of willing obedience to the demands of the Kingdom. Men are to be sons of the Kingdom, not bond-slaves. That is to say that they are sharers in the purpose and aim of the King Himself, and are in no sense unwilling subjects of an omnipotent potentate. Since the Kingdom is not a place or a state, but a condition of obedience, it follows that the subjects share the character of the King; and Jesus' estimate of the character of a member of the Kingdom is enunciated clearly for us in Matthew 5–7— the collection of sayings of Jesus which the Evangelist gathered together from many sources and many different occasions, but which he saw summarized the meaning of the Kingdom when worked out both in individual and in social life. Jesus did not necessarily get up and say at one time all that is contained in these chapters. But we can see in these chapters with even a cursory glance that in His moral teaching Jesus did set the personal, ethical demands of the new Kingdom in deliberate antithesis to the matter-of-fact ritual demands of the Law of Moses, as it was interpreted by Scribes and Pharisees. Not only wrong action, but wrong motive which prompts wrong thought is condemned in the Sermon on the Mount, because it implies a wrong attitude towards the divine government of life.

Once or twice we have referred to parables which Jesus told. Most of His teaching was presented to the people in parabolic form. In this Jesus was true to the tradition of His time, for the writings of the rabbis show that most of them used this form of imagery, though in all honesty it must be admitted that the parables of Jesus are incomparably more telling and vivid than those of His contemporaries. The Oriental had a much more highly developed imagination than the modern Westerner, and abstract ideas came more readily to his mind in the form of pictures. So it was that Jesus came to see the common sights and occurrences of life as illustrations of the fundamental laws of human conduct and divine nature which He wished to impart. We have seen how very difficult it is to put into ordinary words what Jesus meant to convey by the idea of the Kingdom. He never tried to do so. He told stories about it. Even so, we cannot imagine that the peasant folk who heard the stories fully understood His meaning. Indeed, He said as much. 'For all their seeing [Moffatt translates] they do not see and for all their hearing they do not hear or understand' (Matthew 13[13]). But stories stick in the memory when arguments are forgotten. They could go back to the parables time and again and—just as we may—find a fresh wealth of meaning on each occasion. God has always something new to declare to us in the Bible.

Behind many of the parables we can see that Jesus is thinking of the scenes of Nazareth. The influence of circumstances on human character is illustrated by the sight of a woman (Was it His mother?) kneading the piece of leaven from last baking into the three measures of meal;

and the thrill of the newly discovered experience of living in harmony with the divine will is strangely like the excitement which overcame a peasant He knew on the hillside who unexpectedly came across hidden treasure in the field which he rented. If Jesus wants to tell us that God's concern over the individual is real and comprehensible, He does not argue about the fact philosophically, but pictures a Palestinian shepherd who will seek for a lost sheep until he finds it; or a woman (Was it His mother again?) who swept the earthen floor of her one-roomed cottage until she found the small silver coin (perhaps from her dowry-chain) which meant so much to her in her poverty.

Each of the parables represents a real human picture, and that must have made the teaching of Jesus amazingly attractive. Not often did He explain His parables: in fact, some scholars think that the only two explanations we have (those of the Sower and of the Tares) were added to the tradition by later readers or preachers. But the parable-stories were often—indeed, usually—woven round a 'pithy saying' which we find recorded at the end of the story. These sayings of Jesus are the very kernel of His teaching. The fact that they have been preserved shows that our Lord's purpose in using the parable form was successful. For instance, the saying, 'Ask, and it shall be given you; seek, and ye shall find; knock, and it shall be opened unto you', is placed by Matthew in the Sermon on the Mount (7⁷): Luke records it as the 'pithy saying' which gave rise to the parable (which he alone records) of the friend at midnight (Luke 11⁵⁻⁹)— a parable in which God's response to man's prayer is contrasted with human response to importunity. Similarly the parable of the wise and foolish bridesmaids (Matthew 25¹⁻¹³) is the pictorial form in which Jesus encouraged His disciples to remember His teaching,

'Watch . . . for ye know not the day nor the hour' (v. 13).

It is tempting to linger to discuss more of the parables, but there is only space to refer briefly to two which are very important for an understanding of the mission and message of Jesus. The first is the Parable of the Sower, which comes before any other in each of the three Gospels in which it is recorded. It is in effect an introduction to the parabolic teaching of our Lord—'a parable about parables'. In some sense it does more than the other parables, for they are pictorial expressions of one item of teaching: they mean one thing only. But the Sower is almost an allegory of the ministry of Jesus, in which God is represented as spreading the knowledge of Himself through the parable-teaching of Jesus, just as a sower sows his seed. The teaching of Jesus reaches as many different kinds of people as the sower's seed reaches different pieces of ground (and Palestinian fields are irregular affairs in contrast with ours), and the harvest is likely to be as different too. Some receive it enthusiastically, but allow it to bring about little change in them: it never really gets into the soil. Others permit a dozen other interests to take equal place with it, and the result is necessarily disastrous.

The other parable we must mention is one we have come to call 'The Prodigal Son', though the name was not given by Jesus. There are few people who would deny that it is the most magnificent story of all literature; but, when all is said and done, its purpose is not primarily to demonstrate the repentant attitude of the average man as represented by the wayward son, but the patient, forgiving love of the father who never lost hope of his son's return nor despaired of bringing to light the good he knew must be hidden deep below his careless exterior. There can be no doubt that Jesus was seeking to show as vividly as possible what He believed was God's attitude towards the folly and self-sufficiency of man. As a matter of fact, Jesus says much less about the Fatherhood of God than He does about the Kingship, but we have come to accept as a platitude that the main new contribution to the thought about God which Jesus brought was the idea that God is Father. Like most platitudes, this is only a half-truth. This masterpiece of a parable goes a long way to justify such a statement, and we can easily add to it Jesus' allegation that even such seemingly unimportant matters as sparrows which are sold in the market place two for a farthing (Luke has heard that the price is even cheaper—five for two farthings!) and the hairs of men's heads are not beyond the care of God.

Now, the Old Testament had spoken of God as Father before Jesus came. The words of the psalm are familiar: 'Like as a father pitieth his children, so the Lord pitieth them that fear Him' (Psalm 103[13]), and some of the rabbis also use the phrase of God. But more often than not it is used about God as Father of the race, not of the individual. 'Father' was the name Jesus used Himself for God in the very occasional and partial records that have come down to us of His prayers; and in the noteworthy passage in Matthew 11[27] in which Jesus tells us outright how He considered His relationship with God, He expresses the whole in terms of Fatherhood. He bade us prove our sonship of the Father by the exercise of a forgiving and generous spirit (Matthew 5[45]). In all this, Jesus went far beyond the Jewish ideas. We feel that with Him God is always intensely real, and the formal statements of the Old Testament are filled with a new and bigger meaning, which makes the strict ritualism of scribes and Pharisees seem trivial and unimportant.

Perhaps that was what these august authorities feared. Jesus laid stress on the inward meaning of the Law rather than on its outward observance. The dull letter of the Law was breathed through and through with a new, living spirit. It was not that Jesus ignored the Law. Far from it; for even at His reception into the state of manhood in the Temple at the age of twelve, He was found taking an active part in the discussions about the Law which went on in some of the side courts where the rabbis sat; and all through His life the reading of the Scriptures and the general observance of the synagogue worship were very real means of communication with God whom He called His Father. To quote His own words, He 'came not to destroy the Law and the Prophets . . . but to fulfil' (Matthew 5[17])—to impart a bigger significance into what had become accepted as binding. For Him, the obedience of man to God's will is the obedience of sons to a Father. The scribes thought of the Law which God had given to be obeyed, rather than of the fatherly love which prompted that Law. A good father makes rules for his son to prevent him making a fool of himself.

It was quite unavoidable that Jesus should clash with the upholders of the traditional interpretations and with those whose prime concern was with the correct observance of the ritual of Israel to the overlooking of what Jesus called 'the weightier matters of the Law—judgement and mercy and faith' (Matthew 23[23]). We must admit that Jesus is rather hard on the Pharisees in this chapter of 'woes'. They were not, generally speaking, insincere men, but they deserved the title of 'men playing a part' (the true meaning of 'hypocrites') because of the way they went about to give the impression that *He* was an irreligious man. It was their relationships with Himself that prompted Him to dub them thus. The fact was that Jesus' appeal to the people for inward reality in religion detracted from the attention which would be paid to their outward show, though they did not neglect

the inward attitude of trust in God. There was nothing
in their own faith which was not completely compatible
with the new emphasis Jesus came to bring, and so they
had, in self-defence of their position with the people, to
bring accusations against Him which were based upon
details of the *ritual* Law; that is, not upon the fundamental statements of their creed, but upon the interpretations of that creed which had been read into it by the
scribes, as we have seen, in an age which was no longer
capable of appreciating laws made for nomads. Jesus
taught 'as having authority, and not as their scribes'
(Mark 1²²), and the scribal party replied by demanding
why He allowed His disciples to break the Sabbath by
rubbing ears of corn in their palms (Mark 2²³⁻⁸). When
that attack miscarried, because Jesus was able to quote
how their much-honoured David had himself 'broken' a
similar law, they sought to trick Him in the question of
on healing the Sabbath. One suspects that the man
with the withered hand (Mark 3¹⁻⁶) was bribed by the
Pharisees to stand in the synagogue in a prominent place.
But Jesus disarmed their opposition by asking them outright whether their Law declared that it was right to do
good on the Sabbath or to do harm, to save a life or to
kill—a pointed enough question when He was ready to
heal a man, and they were looking for a chance to condemn Him to death.

Throughout the Gospels, it is easy to trace this opposition increasing. Jesus saw, at least by the time He took
the disciples to Caesarea Philippi and asked what men
were saying about Him (Matthew 16¹³⁻²⁰), the inevitable
truth that such antagonism could only result in His ultimate death. At last the chance came to the authorities
when the city of Jerusalem was filled with pilgrims to
the Passover feast, who in their emotional excitement
would be easily swayed one way or the other. They

arrested Jesus secretly after a week in which much of His public teaching in the Temple and several of His parables (like that of the Wicked Husbandman) had been directed against them. One of His own disciples, Judas Iscariot, revealed His whereabouts to them for a paltry reward, and as a result Jesus was arraigned before the High Priest and his satellites. The outstanding feature of the travesty of a trial which was accorded Him first before the San-hedrim, the official Jewish ecclesiastical court, and later before the procurator, Pontius Pilate, is that the accusa-tion against Jesus was entirely different in the two courts. Before the Jews He was accused of saying that He would destroy the Temple. This was blasphemy to the Jew, for it meant that Jesus was speaking against the visible re-minder of the presence of God. (They could add another charge of blasphemy, too, for that was the technical ex-pression to cover His daring to forgive sins of people whom He had healed. Forgiveness was God's preroga-tive, and to forgive was to make oneself equal with God, which constituted blasphemy.) But when the same offi-cials brought Jesus before Pilate, they said nothing of the charges which made Him guilty in the eyes of their Law, for they knew very well that no condemnation was pos-sible in Roman Law upon such accusations. Before Pilate they made Him out to be 'King of the Jews', and Pilate immediately thought of all the violent messianic hopes of the troublesome people it was his misfortune to have to govern. He suspected revolutionary intent, but an ex-amination of the Prisoner assured him that He was no rebel. Then the priests played their last card. They warned Pilate that if he left at large One who aspired to kingship, he was no longer loyal to Caesar (John 19[12]). They knew that Pilate had received an imperious threat that if he did not keep the peace he would be withdrawn in disgrace—a fate which befell him in A.D. 36. So they turned against Jesus finally His proclamation of the Kingdom of God, misrepresenting it completely. Jew and Roman combined to condemn to death Him who had come forth from God with the express purpose of winning them both to faith in God's kingly rule of human life. Outside a city wall, they put Him shamefully to a slave's death.

The clear insight of Second Isaiah had seen that the Messenger of God to the world should be 'despised and rejected of men; a man of sorrows, and acquainted with grief'; and, though the prophet probably thought the messenger should be the nation of Israel or a faithful remnant of it, his prophecy was none the less true of Jesus Himself. Jeremiah had proclaimed his belief that religion was a man's individual compact with his God; and he passed into Egypt as a disappointed old man whose message had gone unheeded. Jesus summed up everything that the prophets had said and illuminated it and enlarged it by His own close fellowship with God as Father, and His message lives on. It lives on, not only in spite of the Cross, but because of it. Christian men have seen in that supreme act of Christ the true and final revelation of the nature of God as love. Paul put into words what we all feel in our hearts, that it was God Himself who was 'in Christ, reconciling the world to Himself' (2 Corinthians 5^{19}). We recognize in that sublime act of self-surrender that Christ was God, and that all through the life of Jesus we are really seeing God in action.

References

Jesus and the tax-collectors—Matthew 9^{9-13}; Luke 19^{1-10}.
Jesus and the Pharisees—Mark 3^{1-6}, 12^{13-17}; Matthew 23^{1-36}.
Jesus and the Sadducees—Mark 12^{18-27}.

Jesus and the Scribes—Mark 11²⁷⁻³³, 12²⁸⁻³⁴.

The Parables of the Kingdom—Matthew 13⁴⁴⁻⁸, 20¹⁻¹⁶, 21²⁸⁻⁴², 22¹⁻¹⁴, 25¹⁻⁴⁶.

The Parables of Growth—Matthew 13¹⁻⁹, ²⁴⁻³⁵.

Picture parables of life as Jesus saw it—Luke 15¹⁻³², 10²⁵⁻³⁷, 18¹⁻¹⁴.

The Laws of the Kingdom, the Sermon on the Mount— Matthew 5¹⁻7²⁹.

Pharisaic opposition—Mark 12¹⁻¹²; Matthew 12²²⁻³⁷; Mark 2²³⁻⁸.

The Trials of Jesus—Mark 14⁴³⁻15²⁰.

The Crucifixion—Mark 15²¹⁻16⁸; Luke 24¹³⁻⁴³.

Questions for Discussion

1. Make out as good a case as you can for the Pharisees and their religion.
2. Can you find a parable to illustrate each of the following: prayer; use of God-given capabilities; influence upon other people? Discuss each in turn.
3. Consider what Jesus was trying to teach in (i) the parable of the Seed Growing Secretly (Mark 4²⁶⁻⁹), and (ii) the great Supper (Matthew 22¹⁻¹⁰).
4. What are the main distinctions between the Law of the Old Testament and the laws of the Kingdom, as shown in the Sermon on the Mount?
5. How far were the trials of Jesus fair?

CHAPTER TEN

The First Witnesses

IF WE are to trace how the news about Jesus first came to be known in the world of the first century, our obvious starting-point is with the disciples. They were a strangely assorted band to come together under one banner. Dorothy Sayers' *Man Born to be King* brings out clearly how different each was from the others. Generally speaking, they were of the poorer class of society, but the attraction of Jesus caused them to leave their homes and work at least for weeks at a time to follow Him on His tours of the hill country. From this motley band He chose twelve, and the reason given for the choice in the Gospels is 'that they might be with Him' (Mark 3¹⁴). The instructions they received were meagre enough in all conscience, and were limited to the severely practical hints which are set out in Matthew 10. With this advice they were appointed as apostles—representatives who should travel from place to place with the message about Jesus (just as under the Jewish régime 'apostles' were sent from one synagogue to another to bear greetings in the name of the whole community). Their real training was gained in that close, intimate society with Jesus, by which He imparted to them not only His idea of God, but His whole conception of life. It was a very free and friendly band. Jesus gave a number of them nicknames, like Peter (which Studdert Kennedy said was best paraphrased as 'the brick'), Thomas (whose name, Didymus, meant 'the twin'), Boanerges (the friendly name meaning 'sons of thunder' given to James and John, the sons of Zebedee, in token of their over-zealous enthusiasms). They were by no means typically religious men. We hear of none who was an official of the synagogue. The prayer they understood best was the new form which their Master gave them. Its ascription, 'Our Father', made them feel that they were a company of men really in touch with God. The impression we gain all through the Gospels is that few of them really understood the purpose of Jesus and the meaning of His coming. It is true that at Caesarea Philippi Simon Peter in a moment of inspired insight burst out with the declaration that Jesus was the Messiah of God; but they seem to have failed miserably to realize the full significance of that confession of faith. Why else do we read that 'they all forsook Him and fled', and that one at least of the inner band had so mistaken Jesus that he betrayed Him to the priests? Yet the fact is that these men found that the friendship of Jesus transformed life completely for them. If they did not fully understand His mission whilst He was on earth, He had made such an impression upon them that after the Resurrection they were able to attract men by the thousand to the Lord whom they served.

Just compare for a moment two incidents which are only separated by a distance of a few weeks. There had been a dispute between two of the disciple band. They had learned something of the spirit of Jesus as applied to forgiveness, but it was with an aggrieved air that Peter came and asked Jesus, 'How many times in a day must I go out of my way to forgive someone who picks a quarrel with me—seven times?' There was more pity than rebuke in the tone with which Jesus pointed out that forgiveness is infinite, not limited by 'seventy times seven' efforts (Matthew 18$^{21-2}$). That incident occurred on the way up to Jerusalem for the Passover. Less than a couple of months later we find the same man standing up in the same city, heatedly denying that the infective enthusiasm which had gripped the apostles was the result of intoxication, and, though he was only an ignorant, uneducated fisherman, persuading an intelligent crowd that Jesus, his crucified Leader, was worthy to be considered divine. 'Ye men of Israel, hear these words: Jesus of Nazareth, a man approved of God unto you by mighty works and wonders and signs, which God did by him in the midst of you, even as ye yourselves know; him, being delivered up by the determinate counsel and foreknowledge of God, ye by the hand of lawless men did crucify and slay: whom God raised up, having loosed the pangs of death: because it was not possible that he should be holden of it' (Acts 2$^{22-4}$). Is it possible to explain that transformation, apart from the remarkable personal hold Jesus had secured over these men—a hold which was intensified and not diminished since He had been done to death as an outlaw criminal?

We may say if we will that the abnormal emotional experience in the Upper Room at the Feast of Pentecost was immediately responsible for their new-found ability, but this is not the complete explanation. We cannot deny that there they, with the strong belief in the reality of the spiritual influences on human life, felt like men 'possessed' by the Spirit of God as certainly as they believed other men were possessed by evil demons who were responsible for disease and insanity. But the fact of the matter is that it was their allegiance to Jesus which had kept them together in that fellowship which met in the Upper Room of Mary's house. The ultimate source of their inspiration was that they were convinced that Jesus had appeared to them after the Crucifixion. On the one hand, that meant for them that Christ had forgiven that for which they could never forgive themselves—their defection and denial in His hour of supreme need. Men who had forsaken and fled needed that convincing assurance before ever they could face men in His name.

K

But the Resurrection meant much more than that. It was, indeed, the final word of victory. It meant that God had overcome the worst that man could do. It assured them that God was King. History had meaning, after all. God was ruler of it. Death had failed to disprove their faith in all that God had revealed of His purpose. We cannot over-emphasize the importance of this. Belief in the Resurrection of our Lord became the test by which a Christian was known. And it still is that. No one is foolish enough to say that it is easy to believe that Jesus rose from the dead: there are a score of problems which are called up by that initial assertion. We find ourselves asking many questions about the particular form of body which Jesus assumed; and we are bound to be confronted with the fact that in their accounts of the Resurrection our Evangelists happen to differ more than in any other particular (it so happened that they were there relying upon individually collected material). But the primary article of the Christian faith is still, as it was in the first century, the assertion that God vindicated His nature of love after the Cross in a way which made all the difference to disciples then as it does to us. This is because such a belief is not merely an acceptance of a dogmatic statement laid down. It is an act of faith —an outgoing of our wills towards God, who has thus declared Himself to us. It is a vital response on our part which enables God to work His will in us, issuing in a life-changing experience which is different from any other that man ever meets. This response has created the Church. The Church is not a man-made society of people who happen to accept the same kind of thing. It is the direct result of God's action in the death and resurrection of our Lord. Look back to the Introduction (p. 7). There we described the Scriptures as the record of a covenant between God and man. In the death and Resurrection

of Jesus we see God inaugurating 'the new covenant'—
setting in motion the new age which came with the
declaration of His Kingdom. Jesus was indeed 'The Man
who broke history in two'. It is quite impossible to trace
the tremendous extent of the change which has come
over the world since the Resurrection of Jesus. Everything of good is in some measure dependent upon that
revelation of God's power and love.

We are driven to the conclusion that the tremendous
impact of the personality of Jesus upon His first followers
affected their outlook upon life even more profoundly
than the virility of His teaching or the newness of His
message. It was Himself rather than what He said or
even what He did which marked out their experience as
unique in human history.

There was another way in which people felt the influence of the unique personality of Jesus. A considerable
number of stories have come down to us in the Gospels
of happenings which do not correspond with our usual
experience of life, and to which we give the name of
'miracles'. There were times in which Christian men believed that the miracles demonstrated that He was able
to do things which ordinary men could not do, and that
therefore He was above all human standards of value.
There have, on the other hand, been people who have
found in the miracles a serious hindrance to their faith
in Jesus, chiefly because they do not correspond with
that ever-increasing body of knowledge we have come to
know by the term 'the laws of Nature'. Nowadays we
are able to steer a middle course. The advancing knowledge of life brought by each development in the world
of science has given us grounds for believing that some of
the miracles which were once upon a time written down
as 'impossible' are capable of a rational explanation: and
whilst we make no pretence that we understand the

method by which Jesus worked in every case, science is making us gradually more humble and showing us how little we really have discovered yet about the laws of the universe. As new laws are revealed, we have reason to believe that we shall find more and more incidents which we can classify as 'natural'. After all, God is by definition above and beyond our human understanding. He has made known to us a certain amount about the world in which we live. Little by little we are learning more, but for us to dare to say that a certain thing could or could not happen is sublime insolence. The many miracle stories which are associated with the name of Jesus are an integral part of the gospel record, without which the picture the evangelists were deliberately trying to draw would be drastically altered; so it behoves us to maintain a reverent attitude toward them and to admit frankly that there are certain things which we cannot yet thoroughly understand.

But having admitted that, there are two things we can state plainly about the miracles. The first is that the vast majority of them (all of those outlined in Mark's Gospel and most of the others) are dependent upon a quality in the subjects of them which Jesus and the evangelists call 'faith'. Take the typical story of the paralytic brought by his four friends and lowered through the roof in the room to the feet of Jesus (Mark 2$^{1-12}$). As we read the story it is impossible to escape the sense that Jesus was focusing His whole attention on the invalid. His firm yet gentle argument with the Scribes about forgiveness of sins (for everybody believed then that illness was the result of moral wrongdoing) and the earnestness with which He bade the paralytic get up from his pallet and roll it up indicate that there was a forcefulness about Jesus which was quite unique, and which can only be explained by saying that He brought the power of God to bear upon the need of men. He held them all entranced by the impressive earnestness with which He dominated the scene. We feel that if we had lived in Palestine then we would have done anything He told us without stopping to question. He gripped men with an authority which was self-evident. It was Himself rather than His actions which amazed them. That attitude of trust—faith—was evoked continually and in many different ways. At the Pool of Bethesda (John 5⁹) the impotent man was quite sure that Jesus could do for him what the salts of the intermittent spring had failed to do; whilst the deaf-mute (Mark 7³¹⁻⁷) experienced the imperative, transforming power of Jesus through the symbolic way in which He touched his ears and tongue and mouthed the phrase in Aramaic, 'Be opened.'

The second thing we should notice is that Jesus never worked a miracle in order to attract attention to Himself or to secure a hearing for something He wished to say. In every single miracle someone is helped, even in the few in which healing of disease is not the object, such as the miraculous feeding, the stilling of the storm, the walking on the water, and the wedding at Cana. May we not deduce from this that Jesus was putting into practice the fact which He was always trying to make men understand, that God's will for all men is good and that evil and disease were quite foreign to His scheme of things? Indeed He announced at Nazareth when He commenced His mission that He believed His purpose to be the fulfilment of God's desire for His people expressed through the prophet Isaiah, 'He hath sent me to proclaim release to the captives, and recovering of sight to the blind, to set at liberty them that are bruised, to proclaim the acceptable year of the Lord' (Luke 4¹⁸⁻¹⁹); and to the messengers from John the Baptist He showed that He considered works of healing and the gift of fullness of life to men as the legitimate task of the Messiah appointed by God (Matthew 11²⁻⁶). The true revelation of the love of God was that man should 'have life and have it abundantly' (John 10¹⁰), and from that point of view the healing and helping ministry of Jesus was an integral part of His unveiling of the nature of God the Father.

In Him all the outcasts and oppressed classes found One whose very presence made life different. A degraded woman gained new self-respect when she was allowed to sob out her shame at His feet (Luke 7³⁶⁻⁵⁰), a Gentile woman from Phoenicia found that His sympathy transcended the barriers of race (Mark 7²⁴⁻³⁰), and the distinctions between Jew and Samaritan were finally shown to be invalid when Jesus made a Samaritan the hero of the parable of the man who was manhandled on the Jericho road and ignored by the official representatives of Jewish religion (Luke 10³⁰⁻⁷).

When we pass from the Gospels to the Acts of the Apostles we find that the infective friendship of Jesus spread rapidly through the Roman world from the enthusiasm of those who first experienced it. We see from the dedication of the Acts to a man named Theophilus that it is the second part of a 'former treatise . . . concerning all that Jesus began both to do and to teach'. The simple discovery that Luke's Gospel is also dedicated to the 'most excellent Theophilus' shows that the same man—presumably Luke, the Pauline physician—wrote both, though there is much else to point to the same ascription of authorship. Apparently this Macedonian doctor set out to prepare for the unknown official, Theophilus, a record of the rise and progress of Christianity, so far as he could. In the first volume, about which we shall have to say more in the next chapter, he outlined the stories he could gather about the life of Jesus; and in the second he traced the gradual growth and expansion of Christianity from the Day of Pentecost to the end of the life of his friend, Paul.

In some of the activity he described he had been an active participant, as we can see from the fact that every now and again in his narrative he breaks into the first person plural. For example, in Acts 16[10] he says: 'And when *he* had seen the vision [at Troas], straightway *we* sought to go forth into Macedonia.' There is nothing more likely than that he should have accompanied the missionaries to his native country. In fact, Sir William Ramsay and others have thought that the vision Paul saw was really a vision of Luke the physician, beseeching him to cross to his own province of Greece. But we must not stay for what must be conjectures, however likely.

In several places in the Book of the Acts we have accounts of the kind of speaking which was typical of the earliest Christian missionaries. These accounts are most valuable, because they enable us to see the material from which later on our records of the life and influence of Jesus were composed. The New Testament has a particular word to describe this form of speech. It was called 'preaching' or, more exactly, 'the proclamation of the Good News' (our word 'gospel'). Peter, Paul and the rest were really 'heralds', 'announcers', declaring something in the name of God in much the same way as the prophets had done in Old Testament times. We can see from the record in the Acts that this proclamation had a recognized pattern: early Christian sermons always covered roughly the same ground.

Dr C. H. Dodd has shown that the proclamation consisted of four parts. It opened with a declaration that in Christ God had fulfilled the purpose of history. It was an announcement of the Messianic age—the Kingdom was at hand. All that the prophets had revealed of God's plan had come to a climax in Jesus. Then the preacher went on to mention briefly the historical events in which that climax was reached: in other words he detailed the

basic facts about the life and death and resurrection of
Jesus. There are several examples of this in the New
Testament. Peter, on the Day of Pentecost, said: 'Ye
men of Israel, hear these words: Jesus of Nazareth, a
man approved of God unto you by mighty works and
wonders and signs, which God did by him in the midst
of you, even as ye yourselves know; him, being delivered
up by the determinate counsel and foreknowledge of God,
ye by the hand of lawless men did crucify and slay: whom
God raised up . . .' (Acts 2^{22-4}). Paul, writing to the
Corinthians, used a similar form: 'I delivered unto you
first of all that which also I received, how that Christ
died for our sins according to the Scriptures; and that
he was buried; and that he hath been raised on the third
day . . .' (1 Corinthians 15^{3-4}). These excerpts read almost
as though they were notes from which the preachers spoke.

The third part of the Christian proclamation was concerned with the consequences of the fact of Christ. In
one sense, the coming of God to men brought a new
accession of power which was demonstrated in the miracles
which He (and later His followers) worked on sick folk.
But in another sense it brought an 'outpouring of the
Spirit' which resulted in a radical change of life in His
followers. It was apparent in the first century that men
of character were possessed with the power of Christ.
Slaves, who had no rights and no hope in the Roman
Empire, rose to a quiet dignity and confidence when they
became Christian. All this evidence made the preachers
bold to come to their fourth point, which was an appeal
to their hearers to repent and join the Christian fellowship, making the symbolic rite of baptism in recognition
of their new faith.

Such preaching necessarily aroused the opposition of
the priests and Pharisees, as that of Jesus had done, and
for the same reason. It entailed a belief that God had

acted in Christ, meeting men even more decisively than in Law and Prophets. Peter and John found themselves more than once summoned before the Sanhedrim to be rebuked for their doctrine, but they were saved from anything worse than a rebuke by the careful intervention of a liberal-minded Jewish rabbi named Gamaliel, who deserves notice also as Paul's tutor.

Chapter 6 gives us an interesting sidelight upon the organization of the primitive 'church'. Seven officials called 'deacons' were appointed to superintend what Acts calls 'the daily ministration'—probably a charitable dole from the common funds of the Christians to poor widows who otherwise would have been in need. The deacons, however, were found to be of more use than was expected, and we read of Philip and Stephen, who indeed had caught the infection of apostolic enthusiasm. Philip, a true Jew, interpreted for an Ethiopian ambassador part of one of the Servant Songs of the Second Isaiah, and the earnestness with which he drew the comparison between the picture drawn by the prophet and the sufferings of Jesus resulted in the foreigner asking to be accepted as a member of the new sect (8^{26-36}). Stephen, on the other hand, had so caught the spirit of Jesus Himself that he died as the first martyr to the cause, uttering words strangely similar to those Jesus had used in His last hour: 'Lord, lay not this sin to their charge' (7^{60}).

Gradually the Gentiles found their way into the new community, especially after Peter's vision at Joppa (10^{9-43}). Cornelius, a Roman Centurion, fetched Peter to Caesarea, the Roman garrison town, to teach him about Jesus. In time it became too dangerous for Peter to stay in Jerusalem, and, after an extraordinary escape from prison (12^{1-19}), he left and became a missionary to the Gentiles.

One of the most remarkable results of the expansion of Christianity was the establishment of a band of keen

Christian men in Antioch, a Syrian commercial centre, where the caravan routes from all parts converged. In that cosmopolitan town they talked about their new faith, and apparently with so much success that they could venture to appoint a full-time agent who should be at call to discuss Christianity with any who wished. Their choice was a young Jewish rabbi who had passed through a momentous experience on his way to round up the few who dared to profess allegiance to Jesus in Damascus. He, like every thinking Jew, had been strangely fascinated by the life of Jesus. He recognized that if what Jesus said and did was true, then the Old Testament had not said the last word about God; but if the tradition of the ages was to stand as God's final expression of truth, then Jesus must have been a charlatan. When his reasoning powers had failed to solve the paradox, Paul found himself transformed by the impact of the Lord who had already captivated so many men, and he became the keenest of supporters of the cause he had tried to defeat. So the rest of the Acts is an account of the various journeys Paul undertook as the emissary of the Antioch Church, and of the potent way in which he set out to Jew and Gentile all over the known world the conviction that Jesus was the fulfilment of Israel's long history— God's ultimate word to men. Acts leaves him chafing in the partial confinement under which he awaited trial at Rome under the Emperor Nero, whose passions at length burst out in a wave of fanatical persecution of the Christians in which Paul—like Peter and many more—must have suffered martyrdom.

But the New Testament contains much more about Paul than Acts tells us. There are fourteen letters which bear his name. How did they come to be written, and what do they add to the developing revelation of God which we are trying to trace through the literature of the Bible? We must picture Paul at Corinth about the year A.D. 51. In the middle of his work there his helpers Silas and Timothy arrived with the news that all was not well with the little community in Thessalonica. There was only one way for Paul to meet that situation. He would write a letter to them, hoping that what he could say on a few pages would correct any false impressions and build up their faith until he could visit them. So Paul employed his first scribe, and the letter was sent by a trusted friend. Shortly after it followed another to the same people. These letters are not carefully worded explanations of Christian belief, but the hurried effusions of a busy missionary, who had to meet a crisis by the most effective means he had at the moment. He thought on his feet, and we shall not be far wrong if we imagine him excitedly pacing up and down a room when he was dictating, pouring out such a flood of words that the poor scribe could hardly keep up with him. But Paul was held in such personal veneration at Thessalonica that the letters were read aloud to the little community which assembled regularly in someone's house—which constituted their only church. They were carefully preserved, and often brought out to be read again, and after Paul had died they became sacred relics of a martyr. The years passed by, but still the hurried letters were kept, though the situation which evoked them had long been forgotten. Little did Paul think when he hit upon the idea of writing letters to his converts in Thessalonica that he was composing the first Christian literature, which would one day take its place beside his beloved Law and Prophets as part of the revelation of the nature of God to men. But so it was, for these letters of Paul were written some years before anyone thought of recording the words of Jesus.

A year or two later Paul used the same method of communication with the little church in the pagan city of Corinth. He had heard that the Corinthian Christians were careless about the kind of person they admitted to their society, and he immediately sent a letter of protest and rebuke. In reply, the Corinthians wrote to him and asked a number of questions about the Lord's Supper, the eating of meat which had previously been offered as a sacrifice in idol temples, and the meaning of the Resurrection. In addition to this, Paul had heard from some friends that there were factions at Corinth. Some of the members of the church there had found that Apollos, who had been sent to them by Paul, was a greater orator than Paul, and cliques were resulting. So he wrote them a second letter, in which he answered their questions, giving them the fullest instructions about the Lord's Supper which we possess anywhere in the New Testament, and explaining the meaning of the Resurrection in words which have become so universal that they are now included in our burial service. He prefixed the whole with a severe criticism of their party spirit, and also included the most poetical chapter of our New Testament, a description of how love works out in life (1 Corinthians 13). However, the situation worsened, and Paul eventually made a hurried journey across from Ephesus to see whether his personal presence could avert trouble. On his return he wrote a third letter, for he was conscious that his visit had not solved the difficulty. Soon afterwards he left Ephesus, but he was met by Titus, who assured him that all was now settled amicably, and Paul was so overjoyed at this news that he wrote a fourth letter of thankfulness and congratulation. As the years went by, the various sheets on which these different letters were written became muddled in the church archives. It was indeed difficult to keep them in order, for in ancient letters there were no gaps between words, no punctuation marks, and no paragraphs! The two letters we have in our Bible are probably made up from parts of three of the letters Paul wrote; but we can deduce that he wrote four by comparing the narrative in the Acts with the various hints given in the letters themselves.

Each of the letters Paul wrote ought to be read against the background of some particular situation like this. We have no space to consider each letter in turn, but these examples make clear enough that Paul was not a systematic writer of theology; and, if we find some slight inconsistencies in his thought, we should not be too critical, for a man's thought is bound to progress in ten or fifteen years, and when he was thinking on his feet he was not weighing each phrase with the care he would have used if he had been consciously writing a book. In fact, at the end of Galatians, when he had been pleading with his people to remain true to their first faith in Christ as he had brought it to them, and not to be led away by other fancy doctrines which had been preached by others among them, he seized the pen from the scribe and with the aid of his dim eyes scrawled, 'See with what large letters I am writing to you with mine own hand . . .' and so made a final more personal appeal (Galatians 6[11-18]).

Some letters he wrote from prison (like Ephesians, Colossians, Philippians and Philemon), and then he had more leisure to work out his message. Romans seems to be the only letter Paul set out to write as a constructive statement of what God and Christ meant to him, and that he sent with a few greetings attached to the people in the capital of the Empire, which he had never yet seen. 1 and 2 Timothy and Titus may perhaps be edited collections of short notes which the busy apostle wrote at various times to his young assistants. But they have all taken their place—and rightly so—in the collection of literature on which Christian people nurture their faith. Someone seems to have made a collection of Paul's letters, roughly as we have them now, as early as the second century, and later they were incorporated in the whole body of the New Testament.

Yet, in spite of the fact that Paul wrote most of his letters so hurriedly and for such specific purposes, it is to him that we look in the first place for the basis of our statements about the meaning of Jesus for the world. Just occasionally, because we are at such a distance from his age, we cannot fully grasp what he is driving at; but in general we find that the teaching of the Epistles is an expression of what we ourselves feel. Paul's was the first great mind to work out what the life, death, and Resurrection of Jesus meant for those who came after Him, and we owe him a debt we can never repay for the ability and zeal which he brought to his task. I doubt whether we shall ever find a better way of expressing the truth about the death of Christ on the Cross than in Paul's sentence: 'He died for all, that they which live should no longer live unto themselves, but unto him who for their sakes died and rose again' (2 Corinthians 5[15]). The most comprehensive term yet found to describe the condition in which a man knows himself to be who is a Christian in the full sense of that honoured word is the phrase 'in Christ', which appears frequently in the Epistles. Paul expressed in words the things that Christians generally were coming to feel and believe about Jesus and His work in the world. Not everybody today can accept, for example, the doctrine of the Atonement precisely as Paul worded it. But no thinker can attempt to express his own belief until he has first considered what Paul said nineteen hundred years ago.

In all fairness, however, we must admit that Paul had some blind spots. For instance, he had no idea of the beauty of Nature as a mirror of the love of God (perhaps partly due to his very defective eyesight), and he took a pessimistic view of human nature (which modern history makes us ready to endorse). But he had broad intellectual sympathies, as we can see when on Mars' Hill at Athens he skilfully demonstrated that Christ was the solution to all the religious strivings of the Greeks—the 'unknown god' of their aspirations.

There are some Epistles in the New Testament which were not written by Paul. One of them, Hebrews, is probably a greater piece of thinking than anything Paul ever composed. You will notice in your Bible that it is entitled 'The Epistle of Paul the Apostle to the Hebrews', but that title is quite an accident. In fact, no ancient book was ever given a title, nor did its author's name appear on the frontispiece, for in days when there were very few books in circulation it was considered an insult if the few intelligent people who could read were not well enough acquainted with the contents of every book obtainable to be able to ascribe any particular passage to its correct author! Paul always opened his Epistles with a more or less standard formula: 'Paul, an apostle of Jesus Christ . . . to the saints which are at . . . grace to you and peace . . .' but the Epistle to the Hebrews starts off with no commendation at all. Its vocabulary is unlike anything Paul ever wrote, and its thought is quite different from that of any other letter we possess. Who the author was we can only guess, and so many guesses have been made that we had better regard it as anonymous. All that we can stop to say here is that the author was a clear-thinking Jew, who worked out at great length that Jesus was the ideal completion of all that the Old Testament taught. The sacrificial system of Jewish religion implied the necessity for a priest to enter the Holy of Holies once each year on the Day of Atonement to beseech God for the sins of all the world; but Jesus, he maintained, through His one sacrifice of Himself in death, acted as eternal High Priest for all time and bridged the gulf between man and God once and for all. The writer realized the fact which we have been trying to establish all through this book: that the revelation of God has been continuous through all history and reached its culmination in the life of Jesus.

The other letters we can dismiss quite briefly. James was written to discuss such practical problems as temptation, the Christian relation between rich and poor, control of the tongue, and the use of prayer. The author's name is common enough, and we cannot be sure whether it was the James who is mentioned in the Gospels and Acts as the brother of our Lord. There are two letters attributed to Peter. The first of these contains statements about the meaning of the Cross such as we should expect from one who, like Peter, had known in his own experience the transforming friendship of the Lord of all good life. The second differs considerably in language and style. Then there is a short letter by Jude, and three letters by a man who calls himself John, the first of which is not in the form of a letter and reads more like a sermon written by an elderly man. John is such a common name that we must jump to no conclusions about his identity. The style of the first two of the letters at least seems to reflect that of the Gospel according to John, and most scholars (though not all) think that the same author was responsible for them. The greatest scholars have differed about this matter, and we can only safely say that we do not know who the author was.

References

The disciple band—Matthew 10^{1-15}, John 13^{1-11}; Mark 14^{43-52}.

Peter—Matthew 16^{13-28}; Mark 9^{2-8}, 14^{66-72}; Luke 24^{33-4}; Acts 4^{5-22}, 5^{12-42}, 12^{1-19}.

Pentecost and the founding of the Church—Acts 2^{1-24}, 3^{1-10}, 4^{32-7}.

The growth of Christianity—Acts 6^{1-7}, 6^{8-12}, 7^{54-60}, 8^{26-40}.

Paul and the Church at Antioch in Syria—Acts 9^{1-19}, 11^{19-30}, 13^{1-3}.

The Journeys of Paul—Acts 13^4 to the end of the book.

Paul the letter-writer—1 Corinthians 1^{1-31}, 3^{16-23}, 12^{31}– 13^{13}, 15^{1-58}; Galatians 3^{1-10}, 6^{1-18}; Ephesians 6^{10-24}; Romans 7^{18-25}, 8^{1-11}.

James 1^{12-18}, 5^{12-20}.

1 Peter 1^{13-21}, 4^{12-19}.

1 John 1^{5-10}, 2^{7-11}.

Hebrews 5^{1-10}, 11^1–12^6.

Questions for Discussion

1. How far do you think Jesus influenced Judas Iscariot? What reasons can you suggest for his betrayal?

2. Trace the main incidents in the life of Peter as far as you can from the Gospels and the Acts.

3. Discuss what place you think the miracles have in the record of Christianity. Do miracles happen today? If not, why not?

4. What real influence do you think the few Christians had in any town and how did they exercise it? How were their thoughts of God and man broader and worthier than those of their Greek and Jewish neighbours?

5. Read the account of Paul's speech at Athens in Acts 17^{16-34}. In what ways did his account of Jesus correct pagan ideas?

6. What is your opinion of Paul's argument in Romans 10 that the close exclusiveness of the Jewish religion has been a misinterpretation of the will of God?

7. What would you say were the main principles of Paul's teaching in the Epistle to the Ephesians?

L

CHAPTER ELEVEN

On the Tablets of Memory

IN A.D. 64 fire broke out concurrently in several places in the city of Rome. There has always been some suspicion about the origin of this mysterious catastrophe, and at first the blame fell upon the Jews; but at that time Rome was dependent upon the Jewish moneylenders for her financial security—for the Romans were the world's worst financiers—and as a result of threats to withhold their credit the blame was put on to the Christians, who were sufficiently like the Jews for the average pagan to be satisfied, and sufficiently hated by the Jews to be a desirable butt. The result was that the Emperor Nero gave orders which led to numbers of Christian men and women —slaves for the most part—being questioned, tortured, imprisoned, and then thrown to lions or burnt to death. It was by no means the worst or most widespread of the several persecutions which fell upon the infant Church, but it is very important because during it the two greatest of the early missionaries died—Peter and Paul.

We may safely say that for the first thirty years after the death of Jesus there were usually in any place where the Christian message was preached sufficient people who had at least second- or third-hand knowledge of the facts of the life of Jesus to instruct those who were about to become Christians. But as the years went by, more and more of these early witnesses of Jesus died, and there gradually developed a need for some literature about the actual facts of His life. In his letters to the churches which met in people's houses in different towns, Paul did not think it necessary to outline the facts about the life of Jesus because presumably they were fairly well known. But eventually some attempts had to be made to record the facts which were known in a permanent form which could be copied and preserved. The result of this activity is seen in the four Gospels we possess.

Now how did these come to be written, and who wrote them? Why are there four instead of only one? Are they complete biographies of our Lord, and can we rely implicitly on their information? Are they all consistent on all points? These are only some of the many questions we find ourselves asking about the section of our Bible which must always be most sacred to us. To attempt to answer them, we shall do well once again to proceed historically.

There is evidence that the early Christian missionaries went out to their task equipped with two documents. The first of these consisted of a collection of passages from the Law and the Prophets and Psalms—that is, from the Jewish Bible of the day—which Christians thought pointed to the fact that Jesus fulfilled the Old Testament ideas of what the Messiah should be. Most of the passages were from the prophecies we have noted already as 'messianic', but some of them appear to us as rather unexpected choices. One which appears no less than three times as a quotation in our New Testament, for example, is this: 'The stone which the builders rejected, the same is become the head of the corner', which is found in Psalm 118[22], where it certainly has no meaning which could possibly refer to the promised King. Another passage which is quoted in Matthew 3[3] is taken from Isaiah 40, and when we were examining the message of the Second Isaiah we saw that this particular passage was the prophet's way of declaring his conviction that the exiled people should soon be wending their way back to Jerusalem round the Fertile Crescent; though the writer of

the first Gospel uses it quite arbitrarily to illustrate the
fact that John the Baptist prepared for the coming of
Jesus: 'The voice of one crying in the wilderness, Make
ye ready the way of the Lord.' We may be rather im-
patient with that kind of misuse of prophecy, but in the
first century it was the honest belief of men that the
words of the prophets could be taken in such a way, in
spite of their original context. A number of these passages from this collection, which is generally called the
Book of Testimonies, found their way into our Gospels,
especially into the first Gospel, which was written for the
Jewish section of the community who were most likely to
be impressed by this kind of evidence. There is, of course,
no extant copy of the Book of Testimonies, and we can
only deduce what were some of its contents.

The second document is also lost, but we have a much
clearer idea of its contents, for reasons which will appear
shortly. This was a collection of the sayings of Jesus—
actual phrases and bits of teaching which people had
remembered that He used when He was on earth. This
would be of inestimable value to a missionary, especially
if he had never himself been with Jesus; and it is of no
less value to us. Now fortunately we have found quoted
a statement by Papias, who was bishop of the church at
Hierapolis as early as A.D. 130, which says that 'Matthew
wrote the Sayings in Hebrew and each interpreted as he
could'. Most scholars think that he is referring to this
Book of the Sayings of Jesus (though in fairness we must
add that not all do so; some think he is referring to the
'sayings' from the Old Testament—the Book of Testimonies, as we have called it). If so, we can establish the
important fact that Matthew the publican was responsible for this most noteworthy piece of work, and he, as
one of the first disciples, would have been a most suit-
able man to do it. Instead of referring to this document

continually as 'The Book of the Sayings of Jesus', it is often known by scholars for the sake of brevity as Q (since it is the primary 'source' of our Gospel tradition, and Q is the initial letter of the German word for 'source', *die Quelle*). It is important to remember that this compilation contained nothing but sayings; it did not attempt to narrate any incidents in the life of Jesus.

When Peter left Jerusalem, he apparently went on a series of tours of the northern part of Asia Minor, during which he was successful in bringing the knowledge of the Lord Jesus to a number of quite important towns. We can imagine that the preaching of Peter would be very different from that of Paul. Instead of philosophical argument, which came naturally to one who had been trained in the rabbinic schools, Peter could bring from the treasures of his own memory vivid recollections of the things that Jesus did. He could remember the thrill of excitement which went through the village when Jesus came and healed his own mother-in-law, and how the whole village flocked round the door of his little cottage afterwards. A man who had seen what Peter had seen has a story to tell, and if he told it with the sincerity evidenced by his speeches in Acts, he would be able to draw a crowd anywhere. He had with him on some of his journeys a young man called John Mark, who had also been a companion of Paul. Once more Papias helps us. 'The Elder said,' we are told, ' "Mark having become the interpreter of Peter wrote down accurately everything that he remembered, without however recording in order what was said or done by Christ. . . . He made it his one care not to omit anything that he heard or to set down any false statement therein." ' There is only one possible conclusion from that. Mark recorded as much as he could remember of the vivid sermons of Peter, and we must presume that this record constitutes the Gospel which tradition has connected unanimously with the name of Mark. The scholars generally say that he published this within a few years of Peter's martyrdom, i.e. about A.D. 66, specially for the Christians at Rome, so that they should have a record of some of the incidents in the life of Jesus.

Papias is careful to point out to us that the Gospel does not set out to be in any sense a biography of Jesus. It makes no pretence of telling the story in order of events, nor does it attempt to tell the whole story. Even a glance at the Gospel itself assures us that Papias is right in giving us this warning. It is the most realistic book in the Bible —one of the most vivid pieces of literature ever written. It was bound to be. Perhaps we should imagine John Mark in Rome when the persecution broke out. The first object of the persecutors would be to capture the ring-leaders, in particular Peter and Paul. Mark had been assistant to both of them. The situation looked desperate. Most of the Christians in Rome were slaves, with no rights of their own, and no court of appeal if they were found in their secret meeting places. Rome feared secret meetings more than open rebellion. The Christian fellowship, so carefully built up during thirty years, might be stamped out in a few short days. What chance of persevering would the faith have if all the leaders were killed and there were none left to tell about Jesus? There was one hope. If someone could write down hurriedly an outline of the stories which Peter used to tell, it might possibly survive the onslaught directed against human life. Mark, perhaps, seized his pen with a sense of desperate urgency which can only be understood if we realize that he would be writing in the knowledge that he and all his friends might be dead before the ink was dry upon the paper. There would be no time for more than a brief account of the main events in our Lord's life, not even for any account of His boyhood and youth. A large part of the

Gospel is devoted to the closing days of His life and the supreme tragedy of the Cross. Mark knew how precious this story was to all who became Christians. Perhaps, too, if the quaint insertion in 14⁵¹ is autobiographical, Mark himself had had a minor part in that drama.

Every now and again Mark slips into the present tense, just as he remembered Peter telling the story. On three occasions he has left the actual Aramaic words Jesus used. Sometimes he makes mistakes on unimportant points which are corrected in the other Gospels. For instance, in Mark 2²⁶ he names the wrong High Priest when telling how David ate the shewbread at Nob. The other Evangelists leave out the name of Abiathar altogether, and the priest's name was actually Ahimelech. All through we can see the faults of the disciples as well as their virtues. We can imagine that Peter, with his blunt sincerity, would make no attempt to paint their characters in rosy hue. Jesus was the very centre of all that happened in those marvellous three years. Peter even insisted that Mark should put in the whole truth about himself at the High Priest's courtyard: 'He began to curse and to swear, I know not this man of whom ye speak' (Mark 14⁷¹). The other Evangelists modify Peter's anger considerably! Mark does not go in for many long discourses. Peter was not the kind of man who would remember long discourses; but he did remember the storm on the lake, and he could see as if it were yesterday that scene in the Garden of Gethsemane.

In dealing with Mark's Gospel, we have not a biography, then, but a collection of memoirs—pictures of things which actually happened, told in the words of a man who saw them happen. In some sense it is true that all the Gospels are collections of memoirs. We have no 'life of Jesus' at all. Indeed, we have not the material for writing one, even if we wished to do so, for the

Gospels give us so few stories to work on. Mark's Gospel quickly achieved the popularity it deserved and was copied laboriously by hand many times. The little Christian communities in various houses up and down the Roman Empire sought to possess copies for themselves, and from one or other of these copies are descended the manuscripts from which we have translated the Gospel in our Bible. It rather looks as though, at some period in its history, the last sheet of the manuscript on which the Gospel was written was lost, and that someone tried to round off the story by adding 16[9-20], for in the two oldest manuscripts we possess, the narrative finishes at verse 8, which is quite impossible, for no one can imagine that the Gospel as it was originally written ended with the words, 'and they were afraid', and without any account of the Resurrection! (There is a note in the Revised Version margin to explain this.) The ending of the Gospel as it stands is really an epitome of the various Resurrection appearances as they are told by the other Evangelists and in the Acts. There is always the hope that one day there may be discovered an older manuscript which will give us the original ending of Mark which has been lost, containing his account of our Lord's Resurrection appearances.

Ten or fifteen years later, i.e. about A.D. 75–80, there appeared a second Gospel, that associated with the name of Luke. We have already seen that this Gospel was the first of two books written for the benefit of one man, the other volume being the Acts. The writer of these books was a most careful historian—modern discoveries and explorations have shown how accurate are some of his statements—and all that we know of him points to his being a man of exceptional ability, with a clear mind such as we should expect from a doctor, the ability to write clearly and exactly as behoved a well-educated man, and the zeal and tenacity of purpose which exemplified a man who was sincerely convinced that Jesus was the true Lord and Saviour of the Greek and Roman world as well as of Judaism. His Gospel has been called by the Frenchman Rénan 'the most beautiful book in the world', and many would concur in his judgement.

We must go back for a moment to the question of his dedication of the book to Theophilus, whose title 'Most Excellent' shows him to have been a Roman of equestrian rank. We would give a great deal to know more about him. But let us suppose that he was a Roman provincial official for whom Luke felt a distinct concern. What a great thing it would be if such a man could be persuaded to join himself with the little company of despised Christians in his province! Luke saw a chance here which was worth infinite trouble on his part. What could he do to persuade such a man? There was only one solution. He would write a book himself, using a selection of stories and parables which he could collect from friends of his, and which would give the stress he wanted to his work— Jesus' interest in the Gentile world, and interspersing them with quotations from the Book of the Sayings. How like Luke to take such immense trouble! It rather looks as though he undertook a journey to Palestine specially to secure these stories and parables, for we hear of several people who are not named in the other Gospels and who were probably his authorities for the matter which is only found in his Gospel, such as Joanna (8^3, 24^{10}), Susanna (8^3), and the Cleopas, who gave the story of the appearance of Jesus to himself and his companion on the road to Emmaus after the Resurrection (24^{13-35}). Later he came across a copy of Mark's Gospel, which contained much material his own book omitted. He decided to produce a second version of his work, into which he would weave some of the narratives Mark had preserved. This seems to be the Gospel according to St Luke which we know.

Such a book will obviously have distinct characteristics. For one thing, where Luke incorporates the story of Mark he carefully edits it and smooths out any grammatical inaccuracies. When Mark describes the case of the woman who touched Jesus' garment in the crowd on the way to Jairus' house, for example, he uses no less than seven present participles in one sentence (Mark 5 25-7), but Luke rewrites the sentence so that it is in decent Greek style (Luke 8 43-4). He defends his own profession from Mark's charge that the woman had spent all her money on doctors, but was worse rather than better, by saying that 'she had not strength to be healed of any'. He omits Mark's saying that Jesus *could* do no mighty works at Nazareth because of the unbelief of His townsmen, just as Matthew modifies the same saying and declares that He 'did not many mighty works there' (Matthew 13 58). He does not say anything about the failure of the Twelve to understand Jesus, for Peter and the rest have become by now names of dignity and honour in the early Church. But the outstanding feature of Luke's Gospel is that the new information he includes stresses the divinely compassionate attitude of Jesus towards people who were not noticed by more bigoted Jews—the Gentiles, children, women, and so on. The parables which are only found in Luke are parables which emphasize that the teaching of Jesus and the love of God are available for all men, and not for the Jews only—the Good Samaritan, the Prodigal Son, the lost coin; and the three parables about prayer—the Pharisee and the publican, the friend at midnight, and the importunate widow. The story of the visit to Jerusalem, when Jesus stayed behind to listen to the discussions of the rabbis, is the only light we have upon the mystery of the youth of our Lord, and it is found only in Luke. The birth story in Luke includes the visit of the poor shepherds rather than that of the wealthy princes of the east. Jesus had a kindly word for the women of Jerusalem who were weeping as He toiled up the narrow street to Calvary, and it was not His professedly loyal disciples but 'certain women' who came first to the tomb and found that He was risen.

I think we shall agree that Rénan was right and that our record of the life of Jesus would be incomparably poorer if we had not this lovely piece of literature to add to Mark's vivid account. We feel that Luke performed a task of great value by interpreting the life of Jesus in such a way as to show to us that Gentiles as well as Jews were objects of His love and care. This Gospel holds a worthy place in the record of God's self-revelation to man.

A few years later, at least before A.D. 85, a third Gospel came into circulation, and this was destined to become the most popular of the three in the early Church. It came to be attributed to Matthew, but it is very unlikely that the Apostle Matthew wrote it. (The titles at the head of our Gospels were not added until the fourth century, and this gave plenty of time for errors to creep in.) The basis chosen for his Gospel by the unknown writer was again Mark, and he made considerable use of the document we have called Q. But he again had access to a birth story, a Passion story, and a number of parables which we do not find in the other two Gospels. We can gather quite a few hints from the Gospel itself about its author. For one thing, his was the most systematic mind of the three. He made little attempt to preserve what chronological sequence there was in his sources, but rearranged the teaching of Jesus and His life story according to main topics, each of which is divided from the next by the use of the phrase, 'And when Jesus had finished . . .' (7^{28}, 11^1, 13^{53}, 19^1, 26^1). The sections are:

(i)   What Jesus taught (5^1–7^{29}).

(ii) His ministry of healing and training disciples (8^1–11^1).

(iii) His nature and authority (11^2–13^{53}).

(iv) The revelation of His secret—He was the Messiah-King (13^{54}–19^1).

(v)   The conflict which this revelation engenders (19^2–26^1).

Then he completed his compilation with a prologue (outlining Jesus' birth and dedication to His mission) and epilogue (describing His tragic death and victorious Resurrection). Thus we find the moral teaching which is scattered throughout the Gospel according to Luke all collected together in Matthew 5, 6, and 7. This is usually known as the Sermon on the Mount, and we assume that the sermon form is due to the Evangelist, who wanted to devote one section to what Jesus taught. It is not likely that anyone would remember for fifty years the arguments which Jesus used in one particular address which lasted so long as that presupposed by the three chapters here. In the same way, most of the parables which speak about growth of character are gathered together in Chapter 13, whereas it is very unlikely that they were all spoken at the same time.

A second hint is given by the fact that in this Gospel the writer makes frequent use of the Old Testament to illustrate his points. He applies to Jesus the words used of the Suffering Servant in Isaiah 53^4, 'Surely he hath borne our griefs and carried our sorrows' (Matthew 8^{17}), and he even tries to explain why Jesus used parables by quoting Isaiah again (Matthew 13^{14-15}), though unfortunately he suggests by this that Jesus told His parables in order to veil the truth from people, whereas, of course, the very opposite is the truth! In the prologue to the

Gospel there are no less than seven such old Testament quotations. Matthew, like other writers in the New Testament, had to quote from memory, for very few people would possess complete copies of the Jewish Scriptures. If they used the Book of Testimonies, they would have to translate into Greek when quoting in the Gospels; or they might remember the quotation in the Greek Septuagint version (see p. 98). In either case there is a very good reason for the fact that the wording of quotations in our English Bibles is often considerably different from the Old Testament version with which we are familiar.

Now to what kind of people would this kind of writing appeal? Obviously to Jews who were trying to make up their minds about Jesus and His relationship to God who had been revealed in the Old Testament. So, though we do not know the name of the man who wrote this Gospel, the scholars are unanimous that it was written by a Jew who probably lived in Antioch (we have seen on p. 146 how important a Christian church grew up there, and how progressively missionary it was) for the intent purpose of providing an account of the life and meaning of Jesus which should appeal to the men of his own race. His main object is to demonstrate that Jesus was the Messiah to whom the prophets had looked forward. He, like Luke, frequently modifies Mark's words, and introduces some typical parables which would be appreciated by those who understood what life was like in Palestine, such as the parables about the bridesmaids who went out to meet the bridegroom (25^{1-13}), the slave who reciprocated his master's kindness by abusing his fellow slave (18^{21-35}), and the man who was not wearing a wedding-garment and who was thrown through the long, low window of the Eastern house—a secondary parable which Matthew has appended to the parable of the great supper (22^{11-14}). In the Sermon on the Mount he describes at great length the attitude of Jesus to the Law of Moses. For Matthew it is quite an important point that Jesus declared that 'one jot or one tittle shall in no wise pass from the law till all be fulfilled' (5¹⁸); and, though Jesus often criticized the Pharisees, it was because they had attempted to deprive the Jewish people of the real essentials of religion by their insistence upon the petty details of ceremonial law.

So each of the three first Gospels was written with a particular circle of readers in view, and each ought to be read with that fact in mind. They are usually termed 'the Synoptic Gospels' because they adopt the same general point of view. If we are mathematically minded, we can represent the material Luke gained on his journey to Palestine and elsewhere by L, and the material collected by the author of Matthew by M, and then summarize the process by which the two Gospels were compiled in the form of two equations:

$$Luke = Mark + Q + L$$
$$Matthew = Mark + Q + M$$

All that we have said about these Gospels has, of course, been found out by people who have read them and compared them and analysed them. The starting-point of all was the discovery that the whole of Mark, except a very few verses, was included in Matthew and Luke, and that there was a considerable body of material which was not in Mark, but was in both Matthew and Luke. These facts constituted what for a long time was known as 'the Synoptic Problem', and what has been outlined above is the generally accepted solution of it which has been reached as a result of the work of earnest scholarship through many years. We did not, for instance, have any knowledge that there was such a document as Q until someone recognized that the material which was common to Matthew and Luke but absent from Mark was entirely composed of sayings of Jesus. We *deduced* the existence of such a document from that fact, and found that the hypothesis fitted in with other facts, and that after all is how all scientific laws have been discovered. No one has ever seen Q, but it would be a rare find if, at some future date, some explorer dug up a manuscript of it. This is not beyond the realms of possibility, for one of the most valuable manuscripts of the New Testament was discovered by a traveller who spent a night in a monastery and, browsing in the library there, turned over some dusty bills on old parchment, which proved to have been superimposed on some of the New Testament, which had been roughly scratched off. This double use of parchment was quite common when writing materials were so costly. Such a sheet is known as a 'palimpsest', and the earlier writing is usually just visible.

There is still one Gospel we have not looked at—that which bears the name of John. In every possible way it is different from the other three. It contains no parables, very few of the healings of the Synoptic tradition, nothing to correspond with the moral teaching of the Sermon on the Mount, quite a different account (though one which is complementary) of the call of the four fishermen to be disciples; and its language is unlike that of the others. Instead, it introduces us to characters who are quite new to us, such as Nathanael, Nicodemus, Lazarus, the blind man who washed at the Pool of Siloam, Philip, and 'Doubting' Thomas, and gives us a picture of Jesus as a mystical thinker who looked beyond the present facts and who compelled men's admiration and wonder by the depth of His insight and the wisdom of His utterance, as well as by His personality and the affectionate friendship He had for all who came to Him. Instead of opening his Gospel with an account of the early years of Jesus or the commencement of His ministry, the author gives us a magnificent prologue, couched in the style of the ablest Greek philosophy, but using the noblest ideas of Judaism: 'In the beginning was the Word, and the Word was with God, and the Word was God. The same was in the beginning with God. All things were made by him; and without him was not anything made that hath been made. In him was life; and the life was the light of men. And the light shineth in the darkness; and the darkness apprehended it not. . . .' Instead of showing us Jesus talking in concrete pictures to the simple peasants of Galilee, the author shows Him arguing abstractly with the theological experts at Jerusalem.

We must not pretend that all these difficulties are easily solved. They are not. In fact, it would not be fair to say that the scholars are agreed about the solution to them; and in particular there is still no unanimity of opinion as to who the author could have been. The name John was in frequent use, and there is evidence of more than one John who could possibly have written such a book. So all I can hope to do in a very few pages here is to suggest an approach which would find general acceptance and which will help us to see the predominant place the Fourth Gospel rightly holds in the record of God's dealings with men.

First of all, there are so many small details such as Jewish customs, methods of telling the time, details of places in and around Jerusalem, and so on which show clearly that the author must have been a Jew who knew Jerusalem intimately, and that probably he was there when Jesus was teaching. He says very little about the ministry in Galilee, and some experts take this to suggest, though not to prove, that he was not one of the Twelve who were with Jesus there.

Then, secondly, every now and again he takes an incident which is recorded in the Synoptics and retells it, adding some significant note which is obviously to his mind the key to the whole situation. Let us look at one or two examples. In the Synoptics there was a story about Jesus walking by the Sea of Galilee and calling to two pairs of brothers, Simon and Andrew and James and John, who became His first disciples. The Fourth Gospel has a story about Jesus, at that time still a follower of John the Baptist, being pointed out by John as the 'Lamb of God'. Andrew, together with another disciple whose name is not mentioned, left John and went to see where Jesus was staying. They talked, and Andrew burst into the cottage where he lived with his brother Simon and his family and shouted, 'We have found the Messiah.' Simon was incredulous, but Andrew took him along to talk to Jesus Himself, and it was then, says the Fourth Evangelist, that Jesus gave him the nickname by which he was afterwards called (1^{35-42}). Matthew's Gospel records the gift of that nickname at Caesarea Philippi, within a few months of the Crucifixion (Matthew 16^{18}). Then, when Jesus was on trial before Pilate, each of the Synoptists mentions the accusation of the priests that Jesus claimed to be 'King of the Jews'. But when the Fourth Evangelist reaches that stage in the narrative, he relates for us quite a long passage of words between Pilate and the Jews on the point ($18^{33}-19^{22}$), for he recognized the truth that the only chance they had of getting Jesus convicted in Roman law was on a charge of conspiracy to revolt against the Empire.

What has happened? Can we not best explain it by thinking of the author as an old man, looking back on days long gone by when he was a spectator of these things? He had in front of him one or more of the three Gospels already in existence, and as he came to the incident where

M

Jesus, walking by the Sea of Galilee, bade the four fishermen follow Him he began to ruminate: 'Yes; that is all
very well; but there was more to it than that. I remember how Andrew spent that marvellous evening with Jesus,
and how he thrilled us all by telling us that he was quite
convinced that Jesus was the Messiah.' Again, when he
reached the bald statement of Mark that 'Pilate asked
him, Art thou the King of the Jews? And he answering
saith unto him, Thou sayest', the scene flashed before
him. There was the open-air dais ('the judgement-seat
at a place called The Pavement, but in Hebrew, Gab-
batha'). The rumour had gone round the crowd that
Pilate had tried to vacillate inside the Praetorium, but
then the priests had played their last card. They had
threatened that if he did not obey their wishes and condemn Jesus, they would complain to the Emperor of his
evil government: 'If thou release this man, thou art not
Caesar's friend: every one that maketh himself a king
speaketh against Caesar.' The Synoptists had known
nothing of this. So Pilate had brought Jesus out to the
Pavement, where the excitable populace had been stirred
up by the priests. John can visualize it all again—the
shouting crowds, urged on by the Temple authorities;
Jesus meek and silent in His misery; Pilate's taunt, 'Shall
I crucify your King?'; and the mock loyalty of the priests
to the Roman constitution, 'We have no king but Caesar.'
What a travesty of justice!

The more he thought, the more the reminiscences
flooded back into the old man's memory. There was that
story about the man born blind. What a row the Pharisees made about that! They accused Jesus of being a
sinner; they dragged the poor wretch's parents there; but
they got little satisfaction out of the beggar himself. He
only knew that he had been blind and now he could see.
Then there was Mary and Martha's brother at Bethany

—we can call him Lazarus though probably his real name was something else: 'Lazarus' only means that he had been a leper. Later still, the old man came to the stories of the Passion of our Lord. Perhaps there were tears in his eyes as he lay his head back on his couch. 'This is my body. . . . This is my blood of the covenant, which is shed for many.' He could see it all so clearly, that scene in the Upper Room. None of those who wrote about it had been there. But had they not left something out? Why, yes. The most startling thing of all, too, as the old man thought. Jesus had washed His disciples' feet before ever they started to eat the Supper. How Peter rose in his righteous indignation that the Master should do the job the humblest slave was usually deputed to do! It had been so remiss of their host to fail to arrange for such a politeness. No story of the last week of our Lord's life, he thought, could be complete without that most significant incident.

So gradually the story took shape. The more he thought, the more he could see from the distance of the years what the others could never have realized. The very words of Jesus came back to him, though it was almost the end of the century now, and they seemed to have gained so much more meaning with the passing of the years. Who could ever forget the things He said to them just before the fatal night on which He was betrayed? It was one of the amazing things of His life that those who gathered around Jesus in that last few weeks hardly realized that the Cross was so near. Of course, *He* had realized. 'In my Father's house are many mansions; if it were not so, I would have told you; for I go to prepare a place for you.' How Thomas and Philip had argued about that! 'Lord, we know not whither thou goest; how know we the way?' It all came back—that and a thousand other things. The old man knew that the very spirit of Jesus had touched him years ago and had transformed his life. The life He brought was the life of men. That was what He had come for, of course, to bring more abundant life.

Whether the old man wrote the Gospel himself we shall never know. It does not really matter; for even if it was actually written by someone who stood by him and put into words the thoughts that came to him, it is still the witness of someone who knew the tremendous impact Jesus had made upon his young life—an impact to which the years in His service had immeasurably added. We must take the word of the experts that the Fourth Gospel was written right at the end of the century, just about A.D. 100. Even less than the other three does it aim at being an account of the life of Jesus. It is an old man's reminiscences, gathered together and interspersed with his interpretation of what Jesus meant and felt when He lived among men. He expected us to go to other sources for our first facts about Jesus, but he thought he could add something to them and make the picture real. 'Many other signs therefore did Jesus in the presence of His disciples, which are not written in this book; but these are written that ye may believe that Jesus is the Christ, the Son of God; and that believing ye may have life in his name.' If it only brought men to realize once and for all that Jesus was God's final Word to men, the old man could be happy, and it would have been worth all the trouble. The more he thought about it all, the more there seemed to be to say: and so, when the scribe had reached the last sheet, he asked him just to add a couple of sentences more: 'This is the disciple which beareth witness of these things, and wrote these things: and we know that his witness is true. And there are also many other things which Jesus did, the which if they should be written every one, I suppose that even the world itself would not contain the books that should be written.'

If Luke's is the most beautiful book in the world, this bids fair to be the greatest. On this book have men of all the ages nurtured their faith; for they have seen in it the record of the transcendent purpose of God worked out as it has never been worked out before. Here was One who later on was claimed as 'Very God of Very God'.

There is only one book left. It is printed at the end of the Bible, and it also bears the name of John. It has its problems, like all the rest. But we found something strangely like it in the Old Testament—the Book of Daniel, which we decided was an 'apocalypse', a book revealing the way and will of God to a people in the midst of persecution. The Book of Revelation is the New Testament representative of this class of apocalyptic writing. It is full of imagery, and the evidence of persecution is not far to seek. Just like Daniel, it was written to inspire the faith of those about to suffer—the seven churches in Asia—to whom it was sent in the form of a letter. At the end of the first century, a widespread persecution broke out under the Emperor Domitian, who demanded that divine honours should be paid to himself, and vented a fiendish fury upon the Christians. We need hardly say that there is nothing to suggest that Revelation referred to events in recent times. The book is a secret document smuggled out of the concentration camp on the island of Patmos for the encouragement of those who needed to realize the victory of the King for whose sake they might at any moment be called upon to die.

So we close the book which has done more to move the world than any other volume of literature ever published. We have tried to understand something more of its meaning for us by seeing it against the background of its history. As we have pursued our way, I hope we have found God more real to us, for that was our purpose when we set out. The God from whom Jacob hid his face and said, 'Surely the Lord is in this place. . . . How dreadful is this place!' is regarded as One who gradually taught His people that His true nature was expressed in the words of His Son: 'Come unto me, all ye that labour . . . take my yoke upon you, and learn of me.' At every stage we have learned that the idea of God has become fuller and richer in meaning. At every stage, the initiative is with God. The Bible is the record of His action. He has made Himself known to us in a thousand ways. We have entered into a great heritage and claim our citizenship in His Kingdom. So we believe that, just as the past ages have gradually unveiled the image of God, so shall the ages that are to be show us ever more of His developing purpose for the sons of men. But One there will always be who has perfectly revealed God to us in the sheer loveliness of His perfect character. We know intuitively that He was right when He said: 'I and the Father are One.'

References

We need to read the whole of all four Gospels to get as large a picture as we can of the life and teaching of Jesus. Below are a few passages which are meant to show the different kind of material to be found in each of the sources of our Gospels.

Mark 1$^{40-5}$ (cf. Matthew 8$^{1-4}$; Luke 5$^{12-16}$), 2$^{1-22}$ (cf. Matthew 9$^{1-17}$; Luke 5$^{17-39}$), 9$^{2-8}$ (cf. Matthew 17$^{1-8}$; Luke 9$^{28-36}$).

Q—Matthew 7$^{3-5}$ (=Luke 6$^{41-2}$), 12$^{43-5}$ (=Luke 11$^{24-6}$), 12$^{38-42}$ (=Luke 11$^{29-32}$—note how Luke alters the order of sentences here); most of the Sermon on the Mount (Matthew 5–7).

L—Luke 9[51-6], 10[25-42], 13[1-9], 15[1-32], 16[1-13, 19-31].

M—Matthew 1[18]–2[23], 6[1-8], 11[28-30], 13[24-52], 17[24-7], 18[23-35], 25[1-13].

The Fourth Gospel—John 1[1-11], 6[54-71], 10[1-18], 14[1-17], 15[1-17], 20[1]–21[25].

Questions for Discussion

1. If you could only possess one of the four Gospels, which would you choose, and why?

2. Would you agree that Luke 15 is the greatest chapter in the Bible?

3. Can you outline the various parts of the moral teaching of Jesus from the Sermon on the Mount? How far is it true to say that the Sermon represents Jesus' picture of the ideal citizen of the Kingdom of God?

4. In what respects is the story of the Passion in John more true to life than the story in the other Evangelists?

5. Has the Book of Revelation any significance for the twentieth century?

Chronological List of Biblical Leaders

N.B.—No attempt is made to do more than indicate roughly when the great leaders of the Bible lived in relation to the main events in Biblical and contemporary history.

	B.C.
	Laws of Hammurabi, King of Babylon
Abraham	2000
	The Hyksos kings in Egypt (*c.* 1800–1600)
Joseph	The Hebrews in Egypt
	1500
Moses	The Exodus (probably *c.* 1450) from Egypt and Settlement in Canaan
	The Rule of the Judges
	1200
	Philistines settle in Canaan
Samuel	
Saul	
David	1000
Solomon	
	The Monarchy divided
	900
Elijah, Ahab and Jezebel	
Elisha	Battle of Karkar
	First collection of Hebrew narratives in Judah
	800
Amos	First collection of Hebrew narratives in Israel
Hosea	
Isaiah of Jerusalem	
Micah	Fall of Samaria: end of northern kingdom
	Sennacherib's invasion of Judah
	700
Manasseh	
Josiah	Discovery of the Law Book
	Fall of Nineveh
Jeremiah	Rise of Babylon
	600
	Judah in exile in Babylon
Ezekiel	Rise of the Persians
The Unknown Prophet	Jews began to return
Haggai and Zechariah	Temple re-dedicated
	500
Nehemiah	

Ezra	**400** Priestly narrative of Law published Final editing of early stories, Genesis to Judges Alexander the Great
	300 Job, Jonah, 1 and 2 Chronicles, Proverbs, etc.
The Maccabean Revolt—Judas	**200** Book of Daniel Gradual growth of collections of Psalms Rise of Pharisees and Sadducees
	100 Beginning of Roman rule in Palestine (63 B.C.)
Herod Birth of Jesus (*c.* 6–7 B.C.)	Herod's Temple begun (20 B.C.)
Death of Jesus (A.D. 29) Conversion of Saul of Tarsus	**A.D.** The Church founded at Pentecost, A.D. 29 The Pauline letters Persecution of Nero—martyrdom of Peter and Paul St Mark's Gospel Jerusalem taken by Titus (A.D. 70) St Luke's Gospel and Acts of Apostles St Matthew's Gospel St John's Gospel, Epistles, and the Apocalypse

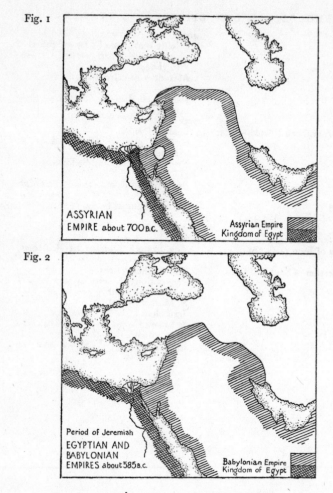

Fig. 1

Fig. 2

ASSYRIAN
EMPIRE about 700 B.C.

Assyrian Empire
Kingdom of Egypt

Period of Jeremiah
EGYPTIAN AND
BABYLONIAN
EMPIRES about 585 B.C.

Babylonian Empire
Kingdom of Egypt

ISRAEL'S PLACE IN THE ANCIENT WORLD

We cannot properly understand the course of Hebrew history and thought
without realizing that the fortunes of the tiny people were dependent upon
the incessant struggle between the empires to her north and Egypt to her
south. This dominated her policy, affected her trust in God, and indirectly
at least influenced the message of her prophets.

In Fig. 1 the northern kingdom, Israel, had fallen to the might of
Assyria (Fall of Assyria, 722 B.C.) whose ambition it was to pit her force
against the wealthy land of Egypt. At the close of the eighth century B.C.,
Judah was technically an autonomous country, but it could only be a
matter of time before she was swallowed by the Empire which surrounded
her.

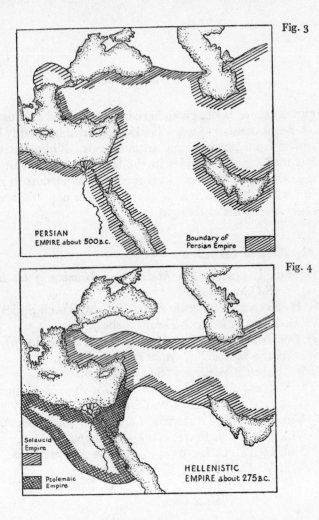

Fig. 3

PERSIAN
EMPIRE about 500 B.C.

Boundary of
Persian Empire

Fig. 4

Seleucid
Empire

Ptolemaic
Empire

HELLENISTIC
EMPIRE about 275 B.C.

This was averted until the Babylonians had replaced the Assyrians, and the state of world politics after the Fall of Jerusalem in 586 B.C. is shown in Fig. 2. The Persians under Cyrus eventually seized the Babylonian Empire and added Egypt peaceably to their territory (see Fig. 3). So the returning captives were able to settle down in another part of the same Empire to which they belonged in Babylon.

But after the meteoric rise of Alexander the Great, division again took place. His generals partitioned the Empire which he had established, and at first (see Fig. 4) the Jews came under the power of the Ptolemies, who ruled Egypt. At a later date they found themselves ruled by the Seleucid Dynasty, for their country had once again become a place of contention.

For Further Reading

THE LIST of books given here is by no means exhaustive, but it consists of a few books which can be readily borrowed from libraries and from friends. Biblical science has made greater strides in the last fifty years than any science except physics. It is therefore important to refer to books which have kept abreast of the new discoveries and movements of thought.

The Bible in General

GEORGE BARCLAY, *The Making and Meaning of the Bible* (S.C.M. Press).

S. H. HOOKE, *What is the Bible?* (S.C.M. Torch Series).

C. H. DODD, *The Bible Today* (Nisbet).

H. V. MORTON, *Through Lands of the Bible* (Methuen).

Westminster Smaller Bible Atlas (S.C.M. Press).

The Teachers' Commentary (S.C.M. Press).

The Bible and the Christian Faith (Ginn): six vols., as under:

    Vol. I. A. F. TITTERTON, *Christ in the Gospels.*

    Vol. II. A. F. TITTERTON, *Christ in the Early Church.*

    Vol. III. C. B. FIRTH, *A People of Hope.*

    Vol. IV. L. C. LATHAM, *Poets, Wise Men and Seers.*

    Vol. V. C. B. FIRTH, *Christ in Conduct.*

    Vol. VI. J. K. MOZLEY and T. H. ROBINSON (editors), *From Bible to Creed.*

The Old Testament

T. H. ROBINSON, *An Introduction to the Old Testament* (Arnold).

H. WHEELER ROBINSON, *The History of Israel* (Duckworth).

B. K. RATTEY, *A Short History of the Hebrews* (Oxford).

N. H. SNAITH, *The Jews from Cyrus to Herod* (Religious Education Press).

T. H. ROBINSON, *Prophecy and the Prophets* (Duckworth).

H. WHEELER ROBINSON, *Religious Ideas of the Old Testament* (Duckworth).

W. L. WARDLE, *History and Religion of Israel* (Oxford: Clarendon Bible, Old Testament, Vol. I).

C. RYDER SMITH, *What is the Old Testament?* (Epworth).

The New Testament

W. G. ROBINSON, *An Introduction to the New Testament* (Arnold).

A. M. HUNTER, *Introducing the New Testament* (S.C.M. Press).

J. PATERSON SMYTH, *A People's Life of Christ* (Hodder and Stoughton).

J. A. FINDLAY, *Jesus and His Parables* (Epworth).

C. H. DODD, *The Parables of the Kingdom* (Nisbet).

B. K. RATTEY, *The Gospels* (Oxford).

VINCENT TAYLOR, *The Gospels* (Epworth).

W. F. HOWARD, *Christianity According to St John* (Duckworth).

J. A. FINDLAY, *The Acts of the Apostles* (S.C.M. Press).

T. W. MANSON, *The Teaching of Jesus* (Cambridge).

BASIL MATHEWS, *The World in which Jesus Lived* (Oxford).

C. H. DODD, *The Meaning of Paul for Today* (Allen and Unwin).

J. A. FINDLAY, *A Portrait of Paul* (Epworth).

J. S. STEWART, *A Man in Christ* (Hodder and Stoughton).

INDEX